Dance Lodges of the Omaha People

T0324661

Dance Lodges of the Omaha People
Building from Memory

Mark Awakuni-Swetland

Introduction by Roger Welsch

With a new afterword by the author

University of Nebraska Press
Lincoln and London

First Nebraska paperback printing: 2008

Library of Congress Cataloging-in-Publication Data
Awakuni-Swetland, Mark J.
Dance lodges of the Omaha people: building from memory / Mark Awakuni-Swetland;
introduction by Roger Welsch; with a new afterword by the author.
p. cm.
Originally published: New York: Garland Pub., 2002.
Includes bibliographical references and index.
ISBN 978-0-8032-1757-7 (pbk.: alk. paper)
1. Indian dance lodges—Great Plains. 2. Omaha Indians—Dwellings. 3. Indian dance—
Great Plains. 4. Omaha Indians—Rites and ceremonies. I. Title.
E99.O4A83 2008
978.2'004975253—dc22   2007048255

Introduction

ROGER WELSCH

I first became aware of Omaha social lodges in about 1965 or '66. I was doing architectural research on round and polygonal barns in Nebraska and mentioned the project to one of my friends in the Omaha Indian community in Lincoln, Nebraska. He asked me if I had seen the multisided building just west of the Omaha reservation agency town of Macy. At the time a social building didn't seem germane to my research, but I jotted down some directions, and on my next visit to Macy I went looking for the building my Omaha friend had told me about, a building he called the Horse Head Lodge.

I recall going down a remote, rutted dirt road and spotting a small, faded metal sign in the weeds alongside the road, a kind of historical marker, indicating that somewhere back in the nettles and brush was the building known as the Horse Head Lodge. I found the building and realized at once that what I was seeing was not just another barn or outbuilding within an obscure American rural architectural tradition but something very different and very special.

I knew about Native earth lodges from my work with Omaha tribal tradition and of the lodges' influence on the frontier sod house. This building was something more akin to that than to the usual agricultural barn (although by the time I saw the lodge building, it had obviously and sadly been used to house hogs). These days, when anthropology is understood to be a science rather than a humanities study, hopeless romantics like me are out of fashion, but I honestly do believe that inside that old, battered building I felt its life still throbbing. I heard its songs and felt the power of its spiritual traditions still in the air, in the wood of its walls, and in the soil beneath my feet. As a result of those impressions I have never forgotten that hour I spent in the Horse Head Lodge so long ago, and I prize them. It is small wonder then that I am pleased to be a part of this important study of Omaha social lodges by my old friend and kinsman Mark Awakuni-Swetland.

I remember my first encounters with Mark in the late 1960s and early 1970s. I felt a kinship with him because we shared a fondness for Omaha culture and the Omaha people. I did not spend time among the Omahas as a researcher, although I was something of an anthropologist. (I say "something" because I was trained and working as a folklorist, a humanistic study not generally accepted as part of the science by anthropologists, while folklorists often do not think of themselves as social scientists.) Mark had found the same kind of—same kind of what? Refuge, perhaps? Home? Rescue? Comfort?—among the Omaha people on the reservation and with the Stabler family in Lincoln as I had found with the Omahas and the Sheridan family.

For whatever reasons, Mark and I were undeniably wanna-bes, enjoying life with our friends while almost by accident acquiring information we would later share with other non-Indian people in classes, articles, and books—or, as the case sometimes may be, not sharing, as we both feel that our obligation to the Omahas as our friends and family supersedes our responsibilities to scholarship. To my mind that is a central issue to the following study of Omaha dance lodges. Dr. Mark Awakuni-Swetland has approached his important scholarly research from a solid foundation of affection for and personal knowledge of the Omaha people, their traditions, their history, and their ways of thinking—the kind of information that simply is not available to a researcher approaching a problem such as this with only indirect human research bases and experience. Awakuni-Swetland has access to information and understandings unusual for a non-Omaha, and so he brings us insights another scholar might never find or comprehend. Awakuni-Swetland can speak not simply to the material culture he studies but also to the people and traditions surrounding and within the items examined.

People like me are nostalgic about fading cultural icons such as the Omaha social lodges. I can still feel the sadness I knew as I looked around at the leaning walls and sagging roof of the Horse Head Lodge. It is one thing to feel the slow erosion of cultural holdings such as folktales, myths, rituals, and songs and a different thing to know that a significant culture is dying, as Margaret Mead realized when she did her research for *The Changing Culture of an Indian Tribe* in 1932. Mead felt that she was seeing the last gasps of many Omaha cultural processes (the hand game, for example) and perhaps any sense of a cohesive, separate Omaha culture altogether. Thirty years later I felt the same way when I attended my first Omaha hand game in a Lincoln commercial building basement in 1964. For many years I went to hand games in Lincoln and Macy, on one hand happy to be a part of this wonderful tradition but on the other sad that my children would probably never know it.

Our obituaries for Omaha culture were premature. Omaha culture didn't die in the 1930s, it didn't die in the 1960s, and it hasn't died as we now enter the twenty-first century. And yet it is constantly dying. A living culture is always dying. A culture that is not changing is not living because culture is a balancing act. It rides on the enormous momentum of tradition—the tendency of our ways to stay the same—but culture is also and equally affected by the inevitability of the forces of change. Community festivals in small towns across America that insist they are "authentic" traditions, unchanged and unchanging, are museum pieces, not living culture.

Yes, parts of Omaha culture have died, such as the system of social lodges Awakuni-Swetland treats in these pages, and yet many old ways continue. Ancient songs have been sung unchanged for a century or more while others are forgotten and lost. New songs are added to the repertoire and will, perhaps, survive the powerful forces swirling in and around Omaha culture. Death and renewal are as much parts of living culture as they are of a living organism.

Cultural particulars fade and die, sometimes with obvious reason, sometimes without apparent cause other than fashion. New and sometimes astonishing forms spring up. Perhaps the cultural addition is only a new format for an old concept: perhaps a shiny CD from an AOL offer for computer service sewn onto a traditional dance costume and flashing in a powwow dance where a century or two before it would have been a bit of mirror given or traded by a French trapper visiting the Omahas. Or maybe frybread from Anglo-American military tradition not only finding its way into Native tradition but becoming the very icon of Indian foodways.

It's remarkable, if we think about it, that anything remains at all of the Omaha people considering the physical and cultural pressures they have experienced over the last two centuries. Just within the last twenty years, a prominent Nebraska historian has voiced an advocacy for eliminating tribal reservations with the intent of converting people such as the Omahas to mainstream, non-Indian, cultural oblivion—a painful echo of the brutal motto of the residential schools for Indian children of a century ago, "Kill the Indian to save the man."

Traditional Omaha religion, dress, language, foodways, dance, and song have all been under various degrees of attack over the last century and a half, and perversely it may have been precisely those pressures that caused the Omahas to maintain those very traditions. Without the exoteric influences that would destroy traditions, it seems probable that there would not have been the esoteric reactions to maintain them. Unenlightened, sometimes malicious, and certainly unapologetic assaults on Omaha culture, language, religion, custom, foodways, and dignity, even as they have occasionally swelled to virtual hysteria or waned to rumor and innuendo, have never been completely absent. While these pressures have now and then been successful in destroying their targets, as often as not the Omahas have expressly or implicitly reacted by guarding even more closely what they consider theirs and what is precious to them.

Awakuni-Swetland's study in these pages has preserved for us for all time one Omaha tradition that has been lost. I feel lucky that on that one hot August afternoon I at least had the opportunity to step inside the Horse Head Lodge and feel its power. But while I lament the loss of the building and the rituals that it housed, I am not discouraged by the loss because I believe the Omaha people and this tradition remain vital and vigorous. And I believe that even as I write these words, there is a young man or woman somewhere who has just met an Omaha who said or did something to light the fire that long ago lured Mark and me into Omaha culture and community for hand games, prayer meetings, powwows, conversations, laughter, and sadness. Thus, cultural, tribal circles such as the Omahas' continue to turn and twine tradition and romanticism, traditionalists and scholars, academics and enthusiasts, friends and family. Perhaps it will take nothing more of an impetus than this study by my friend, colleague, and kinsman Mark Awakuni-Swetland to remind some Omaha of the value of his or her treasures, and he or she will set to work again to reinvigorate or remember them; perhaps Mark's work will inspire an Omaha to set in motion a new breath of air in Omaha ways that centuries from now will be thought of by new generations as the *old* Omaha ways. It is important to remember fading or lost traditions, such as those of the Omaha social lodges, but it is even more important never to underestimate the vitality of tradition or the creativity of culture.

*This work is dedicated to our Omaha relatives who experienced
the wonders and mysteries of the dance lodges,
and chose to share their memories with us,
their children.*

Tom C., Big Brother, this is for you!

Contents

List of Tables and Figures

Preface

Aho, Umo^{n}ho^n ewithai wo^{n}githe. Iye wi akiwaho^n. Duba thano^{n}xti thagthi, akiwaho^n. Waxe iye wi ewebthipi go^{n}btha. Uwachigaxe ti waxube gage bthipi go^{n}btha etathisho^n tapuçka bthe. Iye egipe ke thi^{n}ike ikedito^n ai. Gage iye wi wibthaho^n. Iye wi bthashno^n shtemo^n tamike, akiwaho^n. Idadeshte bthigo^{n}zhi ga thaeo^n thathesta uwi^n thako^{n}ta. Akiwaho^n. Ewithai wo^{n}githe, wibthaho^n.

Greetings to all you Omaha relatives. I apologize for my words, as some of you are elders sitting there. I am wanting to learn things in the Non-Indian style. I am going to school in order to learn about the sacred dance houses. I learned this approach from you. Thank you for these things that I am learning. I am going to mispronounce my words, for which I apologize. If I make a mistake, you can help me. Thank you to all the relatives.

My interest in the topic of this paper arose in the early 1970s. While traveling along the country roads west of Macy, Nebraska, my adopted Omaha grandmother often pointed to a particular corn field near a small creek and declared it was the site of the Wind Lodge —a large circular structure. She recounted how sacred people held meetings in such places, performing great feats of power and magic. Her many stories filled me with wonder and respect for these long-vanished structures and the people who created them. My Omaha grandparents named me *Uthixide*, and encouraged me to "Look Around" for stories from the old days by following traditional methods of asking for information among our relatives. In this manner I learned about the Horse Head Lodge and heard rumors of other lodge sites in the surrounding country. However, other interests intervened so that the topic of dance lodges was set aside for several years.

Entering the University of Nebraska-Lincoln in 1990 provided an opportunity to renew my pursuit of Omaha dance lodges. With the permission and encouragement of the Macy Senior Citizens and other Omaha elders, I began to work actively on this project. In 1992 the Nebraska Humanities Council (NHC) awarded a research stipend (#92-14ss) to pursue oral history work on the Omaha Reservation. The Omaha Tribal Council granted permission for the research on April 14, 1992. The following Council re-affirmed support for continuing research on February 22, 1993. With the spirited assistance of more than 50 elders, a great volume of oral data was drawn together. As part of the contractual requirements for the NHC stipend, public presentations of the research findings were made in Lincoln, Omaha, and Macy. A portion of this research was delivered at the "Architecture of the Great Plains: The Built Environment, Past and Present" symposium sponsored by the Center for Great Plains Studies, April 23, 1993, at the University of Nebraska-Lincoln. A second academic presentation was made at the annual meeting of the American Society of Ethnohistory, Bloomington, Indiana, November 5, 1993.

Much of the information herein comes from the personal memories of my adopted Omaha elder relatives, living and deceased. Any errors in recording or interpreting this data is my responsibility, and I apologize to those elders and their families if I have made mistakes. A copy of the original paper was presented to each of the elder participants, Tribal Council members, and local school library.

Mark J. Awakuni-Swetland
Uthixide

Lincoln, Nebraska
January 2000

Acknowledgments

A project such as this required the support of many people inside and outside of the Omaha community. There were many individuals who provided information, technical assistance, and steadying words of encouragement. It is appropriate that I try to express my thanks to them at this time.

Within the academic community, it was Leslie Whipp's English class which provided the impetus to pick up the trail of memories leading back to the dance lodges. That trail led me to the Archive Collections of the Nebraska State Historical Society (NSHS). John Carter in the Photograph Collections provided access to every research resource at his command. He supported me with excellent problem-solving intervention and advice. David Murphy, NSHS Architect, patiently explained building details to me. The NSHS staff were always happy to answer my incessant questions.

David Wishart in the Geography Department at the University of Nebraska-Lincoln allowed me to participate in a seminar which laid valuable ethnohistoric ground work for this paper. He energetically promoted this on-going project. Brad Bays took time away from his own geography graduate studies to contribute his mapping skills.

The Center for Great Plains Studies staff supported and guided me through the Architectural Symposium and writing process. John Wunder provided consistent, outstanding scholarly direction for my studies. He guided independent reading assignments tailored to the dance lodge topic. John Wunder, John Carter, and David Wishart formed a scholarly triad of mentors who guided me through four years of work. Frances Kaye, Clare McKanna, Linda Ratcliffe, Lisa Spaulding, Martha Kennedy, and Sharon Bays contributed their talents and sustenance on this long road of research and writing. To each of them I extend my thanks.

The Nebraska Humanities Council supported this research by providing a summer stipend in 1992. Molly Fisher escorted me through a turbulent application process to a successful conclusion, while Heather Ropes-Gale applied her graphic arts skill to my Architectural Symposium presentation with fantastic results.

The Conservation and Survey Division of the University of Nebraska provided the initial aerial photographs. Other aerial photographs were provided from the Aero Service Corporation Collection at the Nebraska State Historical Society. NSHS volunteer Doug Hruby helped to sort out that vast collection and make it accessible for research. Additional visual images were provided by Hampton University, Jerry Maryott, John Lucius, and John Mangan.

Within the Omaha community there have been many participants in the search for the dance lodge story. Omaha Tribal Council Chairmen, Doran Morris and Rudi Mitchell, along with other Council Members have given their support to this project. Tribal Historian Dennis Hastings helped me navigate the Tribal Offices, and alerted me to archival materials at Hampton University pertinent to the project. I wish to thank these leaders of the Omaha Nation.

I extend my sincere appreciation to all of the elders that provided specific information which appears in this paper. Everyone's contribution, large or small, was important to the success of my search. I would like to acknowledge four individuals for their special help. Gertrude "Emily" Parker graciously permitted me to work on the Parker land upon which the Horse Head Lodge was built. As the only location containing visible remains of a lodge structure, this entry provided invaluable data. Susan Freemont, Director of the Tribal Senior Diner Program, never turned down my requests for help. She welcomed me to sit among the Macy Senior Citizens. Her advice and encouragement felt like it came from a grandmother in support of a struggling grandson. Thank you, Grandma.

An elder Buffalo Clan relative, Coolidge Stabler, never flinched from my questions and petitions. Culturally knowledgeable and fluent in the Omaha language, Uncle Coolidge helped to steer me through the pitfalls of fieldwork in community history. He facilitated my requests for information from the Macy Senior Citizens by serving as an eloquent interpreter.

Last, but not least, I wish to thank Thomas Carson Walker. When I arrived on the Omaha Reservation for summer fieldwork in 1992, I already had a formal Grandfather-Grandson relationship with octogenarian "Tom C." established through his kinship with my own adopting Omaha grandfather. Tom C. enthusiastically joined me for afternoon outings in the countryside. We traveled the back roads of the reservation to visit other elders or search for elusive lodge sites. Our journeys included plenty of hiking across summer hay meadows and upland corn fields. Tom C. shared his personal history, suggested people to visit about the lodges, and patiently helped me sort out many questions about Omaha culture.

At the end of the summer of 1994, Tom C. voiced a desire to change our term of relationship. He jokingly said that I "did not act like a grandchild," because I did not "cry around" enough. Instead, he wanted to think of me as the "kid brother" he never had. I pondered Tom C.'s offer, and believed it was somehow a result of this lengthy search for dance lodges. After all, those were the ritual places where people re-affirmed their connections to the community and honored the universe. Tom C. was extending the finest Omaha gift to me and my family - kinship. In 1994, to commemorate the presentation of the Senior Honors Thesis version of this paper, "Dance Lodges of the Omaha People: Building from Memory," to the elders of the Omaha Nation, I humbly accepted his gift. Thomas Carson Walker, Elder Brother, I wish to thank you.

Pronunciation Guide

Unless otherwise cited, the Omaha language is adapted from Fletcher and La Flesche. *The Omaha Tribe*, 28, 605–7. All vowels have the continental value. The x symbol represents the rough sound of / *ch* / in the German *Bach*. The superscript n $(^n)$ symbol gives a nasal modification to the vowel immediately preceding. Every syllable ends in a vowel or in nasal n $(^n)$. Some accent marks have been retained to aid pronunciation.

Like all other aspects of Omaha culture, the language is affected by the dynamics of culture change. The orthographic system in this paper represents Omaha language use prior to the 1990s. It has inherited some inconsistencies, including the use of the ç symbol to represent both / *s* / and / *z* / sounds. It also uses the o^n symbol to represent the / a^n / sound. In essence, it is a system that presumes Omaha fluency by the reader. Beginning in the late 1990s and continuing through the present, the orthography is being actively modified by the Umo^nho^n Nation Public School with the goal of creating a more user- friendly system which will assist in Native language acquisition by the community's non-Omaha speaking majority.

Dance Lodges of the
Omaha People

CHAPTER I

To^{n}de gatho^{n}di idadeshte gaxe tamike
On This Ground They Are Going To Do [or create] Something, Before 1890

It had been a warm, breeze-filled day in the Moon When They Plant (May). Sunlight was giving way to the deepening shadows of night. Earth-covered lodges and buffalo-hide tepees were scattered along the upland terraces of Blackbird Creek. Most of the homes were quiet, their occupants already walking the trails leading to the largest lodge in the village. There, in thanksgiving for regaining good health after a long illness, a feast and Wa'wa^n ceremony (Pipe Dance) were being sponsored. Seated to the north of the entrance, the host watched as nearly two hundred men, women, and children gathered for the ceremony in and around the earthen home.

Measuring nearly forty feet in diameter, the dome-shaped room was both cavernous and familiar. A splendid fire brightened the hard-packed floor at the center of the home. Occasional sparks caught in the updraft were like wayward comets shooting towards the darkened smoke hole above. The evening's event called for special efforts, so prized red elm firewood helped throw light well beyond the circle of timbers that supported the roof rafters. Between the ring of posts and the outer wall clustered the spectators. The families that occupied the lodge had cleared away their personal belongings, storing most items in painted rawhide trunks, or hanging them out of reach in the rafters. Visitors sat on the beds that lined the wall, as well as on rush-woven mats and robes spread across the swept floor. The sound of faint singing outside the lodge brought a hush over the crowd. The Song of Approach grew in volume as the bearers of the Wa'wa^n pipes slowly came through the long passage into the lodge. The fire in the center of the lodge illuminated the pair of rhythmically swaying pipe handles, their ornaments of eagle tail feathers swooping like the wings of a great bird. Green mallard duck heads and streamers of red horse tail hair added gay colors to the solemn procession. The bearers passed the fire on the left as they approached the back of the lodge. Facing the entrance and the east, the Song of Approach gave way to the Song for Laying Down. The circling movements of the decorated pipes appeared as two great eagles, male and female, coming to rest upon the ground. After the pipes were laid upon the place prepared for them, the crowd came to life.

Since this was an informal occasion, women gathered at the fire to cook. They remained out of the consecrated area between the fire and the resting pipes. Pots full of soup were brought to a boil while bread dough was prepared for frying. Children chased in and out of the lodge, adults lounged and visited, and the happy air was full of the smell of coffee. When the food was ready, two or three men made solemn speeches concerning their affection for the pipes. Then the bearers raised the pipes with the appropriate songs and danced their blessing before the people. The fire light reflected the movements on the faces of the seated multitude. Bright colors and dark shadows were woven together with dance and song as the pipes moved around the lodge. Many in the audience caught the joy and emotion of the pipes and joined the bearers in their song.

The pipes were eventually laid to rest. A man who had been in seclusion due to the death of a son approached the pipes. He took the opportunity of this community gathering to end his period of mourning. He stepped into the sacred area between the fire and the pipes. With words of affection for the pipes and the evening's sponsor, he presented a horse to a man who had suffered a similar grief. Other gifts were given to the elderly and poor. A prominent man came forward to welcome the gift-giver back among the people, while an old man stepped out of the lodge to announce the generous deeds that were performed within. Others in the crowd stood before the pipes to express themselves with eloquent speeches and unselfish gifts. In this way the community was joined together with the universe in peace and harmony.[1]

This scene of intimate connection between the Omaha and Creator illustrates both the power of ritual, and the importance of ritual place. The act of hosting the Pipe Dance was seen as giving appropriate thanks for regaining good health. The power of the ritual objects and the cultural meanings they carry cleansed and sanctified a mourner tainted by death. Gifts presented during such a ritual took on special significance to both giver and receiver.

The place for ritual is equally important. Omaha ritual seems to always occur within the context of a visibly circular environment. Often a central fireplace is a prominent feature. In the broadest sense, ritual fireplaces are manifested in actual sites along the Missouri River bluffs where individuals fasted for supernatural powers. Eunice Woodhull Stabler, an early twentieth century Omaha writer, described a particular site, the Holy Fire Place, as the point from which all Omaha rites and rituals emerged.[2] Omahas using such a fireplace established a relationship with the site that was expressed through the act of returning to the same location for successive rituals. The act of establishing a fireplace pronounces an intent to occupy a site, accompanied by the expectation of returning to the same site. This practice is seen in the maintenance of family or "traditional" campsites on the powwow grounds at Macy, Nebraska. Claims to the right to re-occupy a particular campsite based upon past occupation are vigorously asserted. In contemporary ritual matters, a minister of the Native American Church is often referred to in relation to his religious instruments, especially his "fireplace" or ceremonial altar. Omaha values encourage a person or family to maintain life-long ceremonial relations with the same spiritual leader through the admonition to always "return to the same fireplace" for any ritual needs.[3]

In earlier times the relationship of person to place was also recreated within the privacy of the family lodge. Regardless of where the lodge was situated upon the Omaha landscape, the interior floor plan remained oriented to ritual activity. The doorway's alignment acknowledged the sun (east), the leading person sat on the west side of the central fire, and the seat to the left of the door held significance. An Omaha person continually moved through this ritual space while fulfilling his or her daily routine. This practice survived in the face of the traumas brought on by the early reservation experience. The Omahas persevered in their creation of space for both sacred fire and ritual. The Omahas built the dance lodges.

How did the people come to establish their fireplaces along Blackbird Creek, thus creating the Omaha homeland? *Shu'denaçi* (Smoked Yellow), Keeper of the Sacred Pole, answered a similar question a century ago by starting with the tribal origins. "In the beginning the people were in water. They opened their eyes but they could see nothing. From that we get the child name in the *Hoⁿ'ga* gens, *Nia'di iⁿshtagabtha,* 'eyes open in the water.' As the people came out of the water they beheld the day, so we have the child name *Ke'tha gaxe,* 'to make (or behold) the clear sky.' As they came forth from the water they were naked and without shame. The people dwelt near a large body of water, in a wooded country where there was game."[4]

The Omahas have never claimed their origin in the Great Plains. Like other speakers of the *Dhegiha* branch of the Siouan language, oral traditions acknowledge a migration from the East.[5] Current archaeological evidence and discourse cannot disprove the oral traditions, and generally point to the Ohio River Valley region as a probable point of origin.[6] Colonial European documents note the Omaha were in southwest Minnesota and northwest Iowa by the 1670s. They arrived at the Missouri River by 1714[7], learned about the earth lodge from the Arikara or Pawnee, and began planting local varieties of maize.[8] Earth lodges were built for village use.[9] The dwelling and the produce of the garden plot were the property of the women, resulting in villages loosely arranged in a matrilocal fashion. The tepee was employed during bison hunts, and while owned by the women, it would be moved and erected in fulfillment of patrilocal needs.[10] The result was an annual cycle of spring planting, summer hunt-

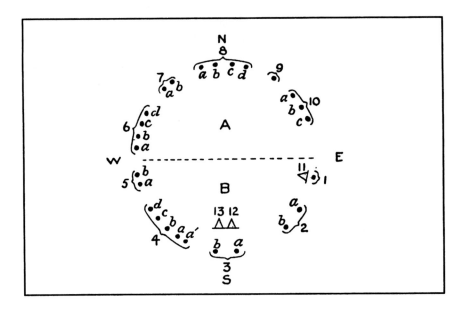

Figure 1.1 Omaha *Hu'thuga*, Showing Clans, Subclans, and Sacred Tents.

A. *I^{n}shta'çu^{n}da* Division.
B. *Ho^n'gashenu* Division.
1. *We'zhi^{n}shte*.
2. *I^{n}ke'çabe*; (a) *Nini'bato^n*; (b) *Wathi'gizhe*.
3. *Ho^n'ga*; (a) *Waxthe'xeto^n*; (b) *Washa'beto^n*.
4. *Tha'tada*; (a') *Xu'ka*; (a) *Waça'be itazhi*; (b) *Wazhi^n'ga itazhi*; (c) *Ke'i^n*; (d) *Te'pa itazhi*.
5. *Ko^n'çe*; (a) *Tade'tada*; (b) *Nini'bato^n*.
6. *Mo^n'thi^{n}kagaxe*; (a) *Xu'be*; (b) *Mi'kaçi*; (c) *Mi'xaço^n*; (d) *Nini'bato^n*.
7. *Teçi^n'de*; (a) *Teçi^n'de*; (b) *Nini'bato^n*;
8. *Tapa'*; (a) *Tapa'xte*; (b) Thunder rites; (c) Star rites; (d) *Nini'bato^n*.
9. *I^{n}gthe'zhide*.
10. *I^{n}shta'çu^{n}da*; (a) Lost gens; (b) *Nini'bato^n*; (c) *Washe'to^n*.
11. Sacred Tent of War.
12. Tent of Sacred Pole.
13. Tent of Sacred White Buffalo Hide.

Adapted from Fletcher and La Flesche, *The Omaha Tribe*, 141.

ing, fall harvesting, and winter hunting divided between matrilocal and patrilocal residential patterns.

Omaha society and world view is embodied in the *Hu'thuga*, a ceremonial circle (Figure 1.1). During communal summer hunts Omahas camped in this great circle on the open prairie. The ten patrilineal clans are divided between two major subdivisions (moieties) of the *Hu'thuga*. Occupying the southern half of the circular encampment were the five clans of the *Ho^n'gashenu*, or Earth People. In the northern half of the circle could be found the five clans of the *I^{n}shta'çu^{n}da*, or Sky People. Governmental, religious, and social practices were regulated by membership within the ten clans and a multitude of sub-clans.[11] A number of political arrangements made clans dependent upon one another for the completion of tasks and ceremonies, thus reducing the risk of conflict and fissioning.[12]

Omaha history is full of accounts of tribal division and re-unification. The same origins and migrations referred to by *Shu'denaçi* tell of the Omaha separation from a parent organization which also included the Ponca, Kansa, Quapaw, and Osage tribes. These partings were the result of accident, strife provoked by ambitious chiefs, or events related to following the game.[13] Before reaching the Missouri River the Omahas may have lived in several autonomous bands and villages. Wishing to reduce vulnerability to attack by warring neighbors on the Plains, or gain control of the growing fur trade, the Omahas were motivated by many reasons to unify into a larger unit.[14] The reorganization resulted in a council of seven chiefs headed by two principal chiefs. Civil and ritual duties were distributed among the clans and families in such a manner as to make their performance dependent upon cooperative efforts. Critical tribal institutions such as the Tribal Pipes, Sacred Shell, *Hede'wachi* Ceremony, Sacred Pole, Sacred Tent of War, and White Buffalo Hide developed over the years to bind the people together.[15]

Interdependency could not overcome every problem. *To^n'wo^{n}pezhi*, "Bad Village," an earth lodge town on Bow Creek in northern Cedar County, Nebraska, was split by marital strife in the early 1700s. The two factions built separate villages for a time, but were reunited after a few years.[16] A period of unification and power resulted in the construction of *To^n'wo^{n}to^{n}gatho^n*, Big Village, on Omaha Creek in Dakota County, Nebraska. Internal tensions, disease, and attacks by neighboring tribes forced the abandonment of Big Village several times. The Omahas finally traveled south and built a village near the Otoes on Papillion Creek in 1847. The tribe resided at that location until they sold their lands to the United States in 1854.[17]

Today Omahas reside in what is now Thurston County, Nebraska, on land in the Blackbird Creek drainage basin they were granted under the terms of the 1854 treaty[18] (Figure 1.2). This particular land was chosen, in part, because the Omahas had been in the region since the 1700s.

$To^n{}'wo^nto^ngatho^n$, Big Village on nearby Omaha Creek, had been the principal Omaha village from 1775 until 1845.[19] Victims of the cholera and smallpox epidemics were buried on nearby hilltops, as were prominent leaders such as $O^n{}'po^nto^nga$, Big Elk, and $Wazhi^n{}'gaçabe$, Blackbird.[20] The landscape took on sacred and ancestral qualities due to these grave sites. Therefore, when the Omahas began relocating to this reservation in 1855,[21] they were returning home.

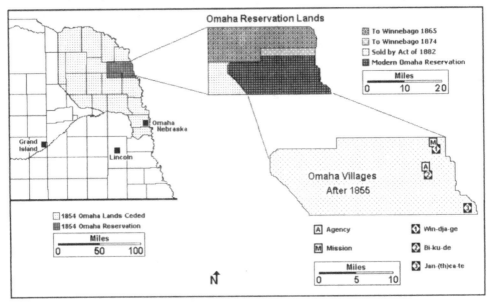

Figure 1.2 Omaha Reservation and Three Villages After 1855. Adapted from Swetland, "Make-Believe White-Men," 204; Dorsey, *Omaha Sociology*, 337.

When the Omahas arrived on the newly formed reservation in 1855, they divided into three villages. The settlements have often been identified by the names of the prominent men in residence. Nearest to where the Presbyterian Mission was to be built in the north was the village of $I^nshta'mo^nçe$ (Iron Eye), Joseph La Flesche. Also identified as Standing Hawk's village of *Win-dja'-ge*, it was dubbed the "Make-Believe White Men" village because the residents built houses like nearby settlers while maintaining, at first, Omaha customs, language, and dress (Figure 1.3).

Ethnologist James Owen Dorsey identified the largest village as *Bi-ku-de*, under the leadership of *Gahige* (Chief). It was located across Blackbird Creek, south of agency headquarters. Also known as the village of *Ish'kadabi*, the people were labeled as "those who dwell in earth lodges." They were considered the most conservative and often maligned as "aboriginal" by Indian Agents and missionaries. On some maps this village is referred to as Big or Middle Village[22] (Figure 1.4). The southernmost village near Wood Creek was identified with *To^n'wo^{n}gaxe*, (Village Maker), and included some mixed-bloods including Saunsoci. It was also called *Jan-(th)ca'-te*, "Wood Eaters," because they cut and sold wood to settlers.[23] By their appellations and implied meanings, the village arrangements clearly demonstrated emerging political alignments.[24] At the very least they were reminiscent of the fissioning experienced in previous centuries.

Figure 1.3 Village of the 'Make-Believe' White Men, After 1855. All the materials used to build these houses and bridge were furnished by the Omahas themselves. Sketch drawn by *Um-pa* (Elk), a village resident, for Fletcher, *Historical Sketch of the Omaha Tribe of Indians in Nebraska.* (Courtesy of the Nebraska State Historical Society.)

Figure 1.4 Part of Omaha village, about 1860. From Fletcher and La Flesche, *The Omaha Tribe*, pl. 23, facing 99.

In March 1865, Omaha leaders signed an agreement with the U.S. government that authorized selling the northern portion of their reservation to Winnebago refugees of the Minnesota Indian wars. The treaty also authorized the division of the remaining Omaha reservation into severalty.[25] The division of collectively held tribal lands into individual allotments was a nineteenth century practice embraced by many policy makers for a variety of reasons. The reduction of the communal Indian land base was viewed as a way to encourage the abandonment of aboriginal subsistence and cultural practices. Indians on their individual homesteads could be more easily led into assimilating Thomas Jefferson's yeoman farmer lifestyle and values, while the "surplus" Indian lands could be opened for White settlement. Allotment would be one more step on the path towards assimilating, civilizing, and mainstreaming the Native population. Reservations had been created by treaty in exchange for vast tracts of the expanding American frontier. After allotments, fiscally expensive reservations with all of their political headaches could become a thing of the past. In their place would be rural areas of Christian farmers who just happened to be of Native American origin.[26]

Mainstreaming efforts were supported by a group of earnest men and women, most working in the missionary field and residing in eastern cities. They made the United States Congress listen to their self-righteous calls for assimilation and acculturation reforms. Proclaiming themselves "the Friend of the Indian," they were determined to extend their "Christian civilization" to the Indians. Organizing public debate and petitions, they lobbied lawmakers toward a policy of doing away with the idea of Indian-ness and tribal diplomatic relations. Their aim was to turn the individual Indians into patriotic American citizens, indistinguishable from their white brothers and sisters. While the initial basis for their assimilation program was the reservation system, they expected to eliminate altogether the reservation, tribal customs, and communal life.[27] Like a prisoner at the mercy of a faceless warden, the Omahas were subjected to the ethnocentric whims of such distant zealots and bureaucrats.

That allotment was a practice supported by only a minority portion of the Omaha Tribe seemed unimportant. One recent scholar estimated that about one-fourth of the Omahas supported allotment in the 1880s, one-third opposed it, and the remainder probably were not in favor of it but were persuaded to go along with it.[28] What seems critical is that the minority in favor of the allotment process and other "civilization" efforts were sought out and supported by the Indian Agent, missionaries, local Whites, and other influential policy makers. The minority view was validated and acted upon at the expense of the majority of the tribal membership.

Indian Agent Edward Painter concluded the first Omaha allotment in 1871.[29] A second allotment was made in 1882, with ethnologist Alice Fletcher designated as the allotting agent.[30] Provisions were made to recognize the 1871 landholders and create a twenty-five year trust period for unborn Omahas. By the turn of the century many Omahas were residing on individual allotments dispersed throughout the reservation.[31] Mission and industrial boarding-schools were kept filled to capacity without any compulsory process. Many homes were constructed while the new land was broken for crops.[32] As they moved into the twentieth century, the Omahas were described by government agents as successfully adopting much of the Euro-American lifestyle.[33]

Following allotment in 1882, the ancient tribal organization (the clans, chieftains, and institutions—presumably) and some societies were in decline.[34] The disintegration of clan-supported tribal solidarity evidenced by the division into three villages was accelerated by the diaspora onto homesteads. It would seem that the assimilation and acculturation goals of "the Friends of the Indians" were being achieved.

The Omahas, however, maintained some aspects of pre-existing social unity in their selection of individual land parcels. Many allottees in 1871 chose parcels close to their villages, the entire process involving only the lands in the eastern one-third of the reservation (Figure 1.5). The 1882-1883 allotment saw a wider dispersal, although many took parcels that abutted land belonging to members of their clan as often as taking land next to that of their spouse's relatives. In a few instances, allottees held parcels that touched land belonging to both sides of the family. Some individuals split their allotment quotas, taking scattered parcels that often included land in the east (Figure 1.6). Allotments made after 1893 continued both the acquisition of remaining western reservation parcels, and the splitting of quotas to include eastern parcels (Figure 1.7). The end result was a pattern of land taking that shows significant alignments by patrilineal clan or pre-existing political alignments.[35]

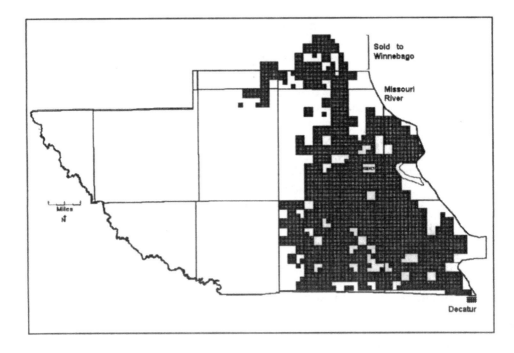

Figure 1.5 1871 Allotments, Pattern of Land Taking. Western reservation boundaries shown after 1882. Source: Swetland, "Aspects of Omaha Land Allotments." Derived from data in Painter, "Omaha Indian Allotments, 1871."

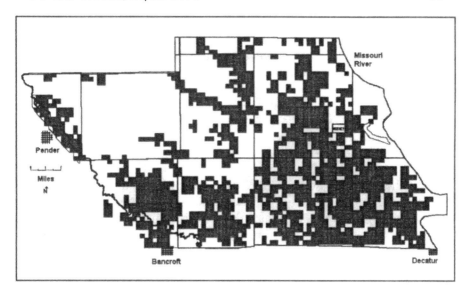

Figure 1.6 1882 Allotments, Pattern of Land Taking. Western and northern reservation boundaries shown after 1882. Source: Swetland, "Aspects of Omaha Land Allotments." Derived from data in Fletcher, "Omaha Indian Allotments 1882-1883."

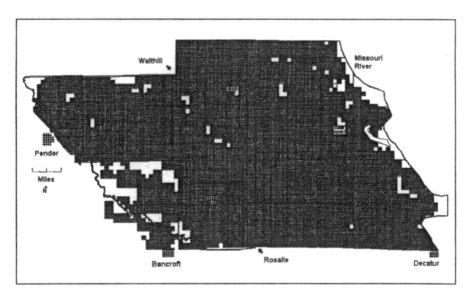

Figure 1.7 1893 Allotments, Pattern of Land Taking, Accumulative to 1910. Reservation boundaries shown after 1882. Source: Swetland, "Aspects of Omaha Land Allotments." Derived from data in Fletcher and Francis La Flesche, *The Omaha Tribe*, 643-654 and Plate 65.

Under the combined onslaught of government officials, missionary zealots, local settlers, land speculators, and the self-proclaimed "Friends of the Indian" in eastern cities, Omaha culture appeared to succumb to a Euro-American standard. Gone were the days of the mobile tepee life. Chasing buffalo across the prairie gave way to farming on individual allotments. Buckskin and furs were replaced by shoes and other so-called "citizen" clothes. Children went to school to pursue careers in medicine, law, and the industrial trades. The picture of an Omaha family driving to church in their Sunday clothes would appear as the model acculturated Native American. But, did the Omahas abandon all aspects of their culture?

The Omahas have always maintained a rich tradition of rituals and dance. Before humans populated the world, Omaha elders recount, a trickster hero *Ishti'thiⁿke* used song and dance to capture turkeys for his supper.[36] Ritual, song, and dance accompanied individuals in their progression through life. At age three or four a child would participate in the ceremony of *Thiku'wiⁿxe*, or, Turning the Child. Through this ritual the child was introduced to the cosmic forces and welcomed into the tribe and clan membership. Young boys were consecrated to the Thunder Powers and to their role as protectors of the tribe through the cutting of hair in the *We'bashna* ceremony. Both of these ceremonies were administered by specific members of particular clans. At the age of puberty boys would participate in *Noⁿ'zhiⁿzhoⁿ*, the ritual fast for spiritual knowledge.[37]

In pre-reservation adult life, much ritual and dance was sustained by Omahas. There were two classes of societies among the Omaha - social and secret. Membership in the former was open to any who could perform the acts required for eligibility. These included the warrior and social organizations. There were no societies composed exclusively of women, although females who had been tattooed with marks of honor were key participants in the honorary chieftain society known as the *Hoⁿ'hewachi*. The *Hethu'shka* (Warrior) Society was restricted to warriors. The secret societies dealt with mysteries, shamanism, and other specialized knowledge. Membership usually required a dream or vision for admission.[38] The various societies, specific clans, or individuals sponsored the performance of tribal rituals. The sound of the first thunders in the spring, the time of planting corn, after the successful buffalo hunt, or when a family raised a new earth lodge, were opportunities for the people to express themselves through feasting, song, and dance.

In addition to "why" a ritual is performed is the consideration of "where" it takes place. The location depended upon whether the ceremony was for an individual, society, or tribe. The entire Huthu'ga encampment served as the arena for tribal ceremonies. The circular arrangement reinforced the cosmic symbolism of the two great clan divisions, of earth and sky, male and female, creating a single dwelling for the entire tribe.[39]

This attitude of ritual space was recreated in the individual dwellings. Sacred and secular societies often held their meetings in a member's earth lodge, performing ceremonies such as the Pipe Dance, War Dance, or doctoring and shaman activities.[40] The Turning of the Child Ceremony was performed within the privacy of a tent set up and consecrated specifically for that purpose.[41] The commonality in all Omaha ritual space was the circular form oriented to the east, with certain floor areas reserved for particular activities or persons. When the Omaha assumed the trappings of Euro-American life, did they surrender these aspects of their culture?

Contact with Euro-Americans brought diverse pressures to bear upon Omaha society. Disease arrived early, visited often, and seemed reluctant to leave. Epidemics, such as the smallpox outbreak of 1800-1801, wreaked cultural and political devastation. With as many as four hundred casualties, including the influential leader Blackbird,[42] the ability to perform and transmit ritual was hampered.

In addition, many cultural practices were viewed by government agents and missionaries as backward and heathen. Efforts came from many quarters to coerce Omahas into adopting white culture. Some assaults were indirect and indiscriminate, the victim being denied the right to see the attacker. In 1869 Albert Green, Agent to the Otoes of southeast Nebraska, lobbied to have the practice of gift-giving and the tattooing of chief's daughters banned among all tribes in the Northern Superintendency (of which the Omahas were a part). He found such practices "[an] annoyance to the government agents as well as harmful to the welfare of the Indians, and that tribal visitations and 'Pipe Dancing' was a source of much trouble, the visited tribe usually . . . impoverishing themselves by feasting and wasting time."[43] Green reported that stopping the practice of visitation and gift-giving discredited the procedure for securing the greatly prized tattoo mark. Having the tattoos surgically removed, resulting in deep scars on the women's forehead, was "not the only good that resulted from the abolition of the Pipe dance visitations." Green was most irritated with "the great waste of time and relaxation from tree-cutting and other agency work required of the young men by the Agent, as well as the daily game playing for the entertainment of the visitors."[44]

After Omahas moved to their present reservation in northeast Nebraska, they continued to practice many rituals. Agent Edward Painter recounted attending a dance in the early 1870s.

> It was a religious one, held in a mud lodge. The Indians were seated around the fire in the center of the lodge. They were painted in the most hideous manner, and decorated with feathers and many kinds of war trappings. When the dance began, with wild savage gestures and unearthly yells, my Catholic relative grasped the crucifix at her side, and with a look of terror on her face held it to her lips, muttering long prayers, until a chance for making our exit appeared.[45]

His ethnocentric indignation at Omaha culture coincided with that of most agents and missionaries sent to administer the tribe. Those individuals used their position to pressure Omahas into abandoning many of their customs in favor of Euro-American practices.

The ethnographer who so movingly described the WaWa[n] Pipe Dance she sponsored on a May evening in 1884, spent most of her energy trying to dismantle the society that supported such ritual. Alice Fletcher came to the Omahas in 1881 with the intention of studying their culture. Her position as an ethnographer was often at odds with her participation in the programs and goals of "the Friends of the Indian." In 1882 she helped a group of so-called "progressive" Omahas present a petition to Congress calling for the communal tribal lands to be allotted to individuals.[46] Designated as the agent for the United States government, Fletcher spent the following two years encouraging the diaspora of the Omahas away from their traditional village life.[47] At the same time she bundled children off to boarding schools at Carlisle Indian School, Pennsylvania, and Hampton Institute, Virginia.[48] The Omahas were guided to dispersal into isolated farmsteads, the adults were discouraged from maintaining ancient rituals, and the children were forcibly indoctrinated into American society. By 1884 Fletcher had overseen the allotment of 75,931 acres in 954 separate parcels to 1,194 persons. As the number of allottees exceeded the official 1884 agency census by 27 persons, it appears that the division of communal reservation land into individual tracts was thorough.[49]

By the end of the nineteenth century Omahas had indeed adopted much of the clothing, dwellings, and social practices of their white neighbors, but Omaha resistance to this cultural replacement also occurred. Individual ethnic and ritual expressions such as the display of a woman's Mark of Honor tattoos could be effectively hidden from non-Omaha scrutiny (Figures 1.8, 1.9). Larger ritual processes required other adaptive strategies.

Figure 1.8 Mark of Honor, displayed. Mary Mitchell McCauley (Courtesy Nebraska State Historical Society, photo no. RG3882:56-11).

Figure 1.9 Mark of Honor, discretely concealed from the non-Omaha public.
Mary Mitchell McCauley shaking hands with Governor Weaver (Courtesy
Nebraska State Historical Society, photo no. RG3882:58-1).

At the close of the nineteenth century a new wooden structure appeared among some Omaha homesteads. Shake shingled roof on a clapboard wall, these circular barn-like buildings seemed reminiscent of the recently abandoned earth lodges. Camouflaged in the architectural styles of their Euro-American neighbors, these were the dance lodges of private individuals, secret societies, and social organizations. Omaha ritual and dance had not been stamped out by the missionaries and government agents. Instead, it had adopted some of the external clothing that would allow it to blend in with the surrounding countryside.

Circular wooden structures are not unique to the Omaha. A variety of such structures could be found in the late nineteenth and early twentieth century among other Great Plains tribes, including the Ponca, Osage, Pawnee, Gros Ventre, and several Sioux groups.[50] Existing studies of these groups do not uniformly offer in-depth ethnohistorical descriptions of the lodges. A cross-cultural comparative study remains to be conducted. This current investigation of the Omaha lodges contributes to that much needed larger study.

Multiple Omaha dance lodges were built and maintained from the turn of the century through the 1940s. Were these lodges preserving Omaha culture and an expression of resistance, or were they evidence of cultural innovation and change? Who was responsible for their emergence, and for what purpose? These questions will be answered when we look more closely at the years 1890 to 1930. That was the time when the "*xube'wachigaxe*," the time when the sacred people danced.

NOTES

1. Alice C. Fletcher, "Personal Studies of Indian Life: Politics and 'Pipe-Dancing'," *The Century Magazine*, 45(1893):454–455.

2. Stephen Cobb, et al, editors, *La-ta-we-sah (Woman of the Bird clan): Her Poetry and Prose*, (Macy, Nebraska: Macy School Press, 1989), 24. La-ta-we-sah, Eunice Woodhull Stabler(1885–1963), has been described as both a traditional Omaha woman and a college educated poet and writer. She is best known for her collection of writings in *How Beautiful the Land of My Forefathers*, (privately printed, 1943); Reo F. Fortune, *Omaha Secret Societies*, reprinted 1932 (New York: A.M.S. Press, 1969), 41.

3. Mark J. Swetland, "A Few Words Concerning the Fireplace at the Lincoln Indian Center, 1100 Military Road, Lincoln, Nebraska." Typescript in the author's possession, 1985.

4. Alice C. Fletcher and Francis La Flesche, *The Omaha Tribe*, Twenty-Seventh Annual Report of the Bureau of American Ethnology, 1905–1906 (Washington: Government Printing Office, 1911), 70.

5. Ibid., 70–72.

6. Susan C. Vehik, "Dhegiha Origins and Plains Archaeology," *Plains Anthropologist* 38/146 (1993): 231–252.

7. John M. O'Shea and John Ludwickson, *Archaeology and Ethnohistory of the Omaha Indians: The Big Village Site* (Lincoln: University of Nebraska Press, 1992), 17, 72, 77.

8. Fletcher and La Flesche, *The Omaha Tribe*, 75–76.

9. Ibid., 76.

10. Frederick Dean McEvoy, "A Thesis: Reservation Settlement Patterns of the Omaha Indians, 1854–1930," (Honors Thesis, Department of Anthropology, University of Nebraska-Lincoln, 1963), 6.

11. Fletcher and La Flesche, *The Omaha Tribe*,134–141.

12. Margaret Mead, *The Changing Culture of an Indian Tribe* (New York: Columbia University Press, 1932), 62.

13. Fletcher and La Flesche, *The Omaha Tribe*, 38.

14. John M. O'Shea and John Ludwickson, *Archaeology and Ethnohistory of the Omaha Indians*, 17–18.

15. Fletcher and La Flesche, *The Omaha Tribe*, 199–202, 217–219, 251–260; For a more contemporary summary and interpretation of these tribal institutions and activities see Robin Ridington and Dennis Hastings *Blessing for a Long Time: The Sacred Pole of the Omaha Tribe* (Lincoln: University of Nebraska Press, 1997).

16. Fletcher and La Flesche, *The Omaha Tribe*, 85–86.

17. Ibid., 99–100.

18. Charles Royce, *Indian Land Cessions in the United States* (Washington: Government Printing Office, 1900), 791.

19. O'Shea and Ludwickson, *Archaeology and Ethnohistory of the Omaha Indians*, 1.

20. Fletcher and La Flesche, *The Omaha Tribe*, 83–86.

21. James Owen Dorsey, *Omaha Sociology*, Third Annual Report of the Bureau of American Ethnology, 1881–1882 (Washington: Government Printing Office, 1884), 214.

22. David J. Wishart, *An Unspeakable Sadness: The Dispossession of the Nebraska Indians*, 1994 (Lincoln: University of Nebraska Press), 120–1.

23. Dorsey, *Omaha Sociology*, 337; Francis La Flesche, *The Middle Five: Indian Schoolboys of the Omaha Tribe* (1900; reprint, Lincoln: University of Nebraska Press, 1963), pp. xix–xx. Other spellings include *Jan-(th)ca'-te*, *Ton'-won-ga-hae*, *Ish'-ka-da-be*, and *E-sta'-ma-za*; "Wood Eaters," was also attributed to an insect found under the bark of trees. Dorsey, Omaha Dwellings, Furniture, and Implements, 270–1.

24. McEvoy, "Reservation Settlement Patterns," 18.

25. Charles J. Kappler, *Treaties,—Indian Affairs: Laws and Treaties*, 4 vols. (Washington: Government Printing Office, 1904), 2:872–873.

26. Recent scholarly work on the allotment process and its multi-faceted impacts on contemporary Omaha culture and society can be found in Joan Mark, *A Stranger in Her Native Land: Alice Fletcher and the American Indians* (Lincoln: University of Nebraska Press, 1988); Judith Boughter, *Betraying the Omaha Nation, 1790–1916* (Norman: University of Oklahoma Press, 1998); Mark Scherer, *Imperfect Victories: The Legal Tenacity of the Omaha Tribe, 1945–1995* (Lincoln: University of Nebraska Press, 1999); Wishart, *An Unspeakable Sadness*.

27. Francis Paul Prucha, *The Great Father: The United States Government and the American Indian*, 2 vols. (Lincoln: University of Nebraska Press, 1984), 2:609–610.

28. Mark, *A Stranger in Her Native Land*, 93., Boughter, *Betraying the Omaha Nation, 1790–1916*, 90.

29. Edward Painter, "Omaha Indian Allotments, 1871," Microfilm RG508, Roll No. 120, Nebraska State Historical Society, Lincoln, Nebraska. This document listed 331 allotments signed on 23 December 1870. Each numbered entry included an English name, Omaha name, gender, age, section, township, range, and total acres allotted. A number of the entries had an overstrike with the notation "Winnebago," indicating allotted parcels that became part of the Winnebago Reservation after 1865.

30. Alice C. Fletcher, "Omaha Indian Allotments, 1882–1883," Great Plains Art Collection, Center for Great Plains Studies, University of Nebraska-Lincoln. This document includes 203 pages of indexed entries. Roughly grouped by family units, each entry includes either an English name, an Omaha name, or both. Age, kinship, section, township, and range are provided. Some entries include the number of acres broken and type of dwelling on the allotment.

31. Kappler, *Treaties* 1:212–214.

32. *Annual Report of the Commissioner of Indian Affairs, For the Year 1887* (Washington: Government Printing Office, 1887), 153. Hereinafter ARCIA.

33. Ibid.,152–153.

34. Fletcher and La Flesche, *The Omaha Tribe*, 33.

35. Mark J. Swetland, "Aspect of Omaha Land Allotments, 1855–1910: With Reference to a Series of Three Maps." Typescript in the author's possession, 1992.

36. James Owen Dorsey, *The egiha Language*, U.S. Geographical and Geological Survey of the Rocky Mountain Region, Contributions to North American Ethnology (Washington: Government Printing Office, 1890), 6:60–65.

37. Fletcher and La Flesche, *The Omaha Tribe*, 117–133.

38. Ibid., 459–460.

39. Ibid., 38.

40. Ibid., 460.

41. Ibid., 118.

42. O'Shea and Ludwickson, *Archaeology and Ethnohistory of the Omaha Indians,* 30.

43. Albert Lamborn Green, "The Language and Customs of a Nearly Extinct Nation of Ancient Quivera Whose Component Bands Still Survive and Are Known as the Otoes, Iowas, and Missouris," ms, 2800, Nebraska State Historical Society, Lincoln, Nebraska, 68–70. Green was Indian Agent from 1869 through 1872. The document is inscribed "May 1939."

44. Ibid., 70.

45. Orrin C. Painter, *William Painter and His Father Dr. Edward Painter: Sketches and Reminiscences* (Baltimore: The Arundel Press, 1914), 141–142.

46. Alice C. Fletcher, (Editor) "Memorial of the Members of the Omaha Tribe of Indians for a Grant of Land in Severalty." 47th Congress, 1st Session, *Senate Miscellaneous Documents,* no. 31. 1882.

47. Alice C. Fletcher, *Lands in Severalty to Indians: Illustrated by Experiences With The Omaha Tribe,* (Salem, MA: Salem Press, 1885), 9.

48. Mark, *A Stranger in Her Native Land,* 79–86.

49. ARCIA (Washington: Government Printing Office, 1884), 118, 294.

50. For example, photographs or brief descriptions of circular wooden lodges similar to the Omaha type can be found in James H. Howard, *The Ponca Tribe,* Smithsonian Institution, Bureau of American Ethnology Bulletin 195. Washington, DC: Government Printing Office, 1965; Alice Anne Callahan, *The Osage Ceremonial Dance I'n-Lon-Schka,* Norman: University of Oklahoma Press, 1990; Frances Densmore, *Pawnee Music,* Smithsonian Institution, Bureau of American Ethnology Bulletin 93. Washington, DC: Government Printing Office, 1929; John A. Anderson, Henry W. Hamilton, and Jean Tyree Hamilton, *The Sioux of the Rosebud: A History in Pictures,* Norman: University of Oklahoma Press, 1971; and Loretta Fowler, *Shared Symbols, Contested Meanings: Gros Ventre Culture and History, 1778–1984,* Ithaca: Cornell University Press, 1987.

CHAPTER II

Pahoⁿgadiamoⁿ waxube uwachigaxe ai gatha:

From the Beginning They Had Sacred Dancing, 1890–1930

It was near the end of the Moon When The Little Black Bears Are Born (December). The sun reached its southernmost point, and started the long trip back toward the land of the Omahas. While its light reflected brightly on the fresh snowdrifts surrounding a new building, it provided little warmth against the freezing Nebraska winds. Many families had traveled from neighboring farmsteads to take part in the festivities at the Wind Lodge. Young male relatives split wood for the outside cooking fire and the heating stove inside the circular wooden lodge. Everyone brought warm blankets to sit on the floor and for bundling sleepy children during the late-night wagon ride home. Since it was called "Christmas," a cedar tree had been decorated with candles and erected inside the lodge. However, the ensuing War Dance was so exciting that everyone forgot to watch the tree. In the middle of the merrymaking the candles caught the tree on fire. That dance was remembered "as the time when the people threw the Christmas tree out of the lodge onto a snow bank."[1]

During the Nebraska Historical Society's 1905 expedition to the Omaha Reservation, Director Addison E. Sheldon took a photograph of his young son mounted on a horse, while posed in front of a circular structure (Figure 2.1). Other than identifying the building as a dance lodge, Sheldon's notes do not provide any description of its location, dimensions, or significance. A pair of painted horse heads ornamenting the dance lodge door, gaze out of one of the earliest and rare photographs of this type of structure.[2]

Figure 2.1 Horse Head Lodge, 1905. Phillip Sheldon posed on a horse. Note the untrimmed shingles over the left (north) window, and the pair of painted horse heads on the door. Photograph by Addison E. Sheldon. (Courtesy Nebraska State Historical Society, photo no. RG2039:15).

In 1911 Alice Fletcher and Francis La Flesche published their ethnography of the Omahas that included descriptions of several secret societies at the turn of the century. Two societies most often identified with dance lodges were the *Washish'ka athin*, and the *In'kugthin athin*. The *Washish'ka athin*, or Shell Society, was associated with the ability to heal sickness by means of herbs and roots. A knowledge of these roots and herbs had been given to the society founders by a mysterious stranger, who was the messenger of the council of animals that dwelt in a great lake. The society was organized in order to preserve the story upon which it was founded, and the dramatic re-enactment of this creation story formed the basis of the ceremonies observed at regular meetings. Members wore gaily ornamented regalia. Floor plans for meetings followed an earth lodge pattern, while their use of a "circular wooden building arranged like the latter" was noted.[3] Six photographs of Shell Society members taken inside a dance lodge accompanied the report. Five of the six had been retouched, probably to enhance the dancers, by removing the distracting details of the building from the background [4] (Figures 2.2, 2.3).

Figure 2.2 Members of the Shell Society, before 1910. Note the background has been obscured for publication purposes. From Fletcher and La Flesche, *The Omaha Tribe*, pl. 64, facing 519 (Courtesy National Anthropological Archives, Smithsonian Institution).

Figure 2.3 Members of the Shell Society, before 1910. Original image prior to retouching for publication in Fletcher and La Flesche, *The Omaha Tribe*, pl. 64, facing 519. Note the window covered by a piece of cloth visible in the background and the interior wall construction details. (courtesy National Anthropological Archives, Smithsonian Institution, photo no. 92-16948).

An older lodge-based secret organization, the *I^n'kugthi^n athi^n*, Pebble or Marble Society, was briefly discussed by Fletcher and La Flesche. Members of the society treated sickness by mechanical means—bleeding, sucking out the disturbing object, and massaging the area below the ribs. Membership was gained by virtue of a dream, or vision, of water or its representative, the pebble, or the water monster. Pebble Society members wore little elaborate clothing during ceremonies, but relied upon body paint to depict animals seen in personal dreams. The public part of the ceremony included demonstrations of mysterious power. Members took turns "shooting" each other with ritual projectiles, usually small pebbles withdrawn from inside their bodies. Persons struck by these mysterious projectiles were "killed" and fell to the ground. They would then be "revived" as proof of the society's power to heal. Meetings were held in a member's lodge, usually occurring only through summer.[5]

In 1930 anthropologist Margaret Mead characterized the Omaha and other Plains Indian cultures as broken and dying. Her work on the reservation in 1930 was performed without utilizing the native language,[6] and she produced a generally pessimistic report on Omaha culture in transition. Concentrating upon women in the society, the subject of dance lodges received only passing mention. Fictitious place names were used to preserve anonymity. Mead identified the following lodges: the Buffalo Lodge, Little Deer Lodge, Rainbow Lodge, and the Badger Lodge. Membership was reportedly informal and based upon habitual attendance.[7]

There is little Euro-American documentation of the emerging dance lodges. It is the experiences and memories of today's Omaha elders that preserve a more complete story.[8] Their first answer to any question about dance lodges was nearly always a uniform reply, "That was where the *xube wachigaxe* (sacred people danced)." They described how only secret society members and invited guests could attend the sacred dances. Unlike other social activities where leftover food could be taken home, the food that was prepared for a sacred dance was consumed on the spot. Children who could not sit quietly in the lodge were left to play outside among the tethered horses and wagons. Casual conversation about the secret society rituals is frowned upon today. The salient point is the strong association of the dance lodge with the maintenance of sacred power, ritual, and Omaha cultural survival.

Further discussions with elders about these structures broadened into stories about their use by neighborhood social organizations, such as the turn-of-the-century Christmas dance at the Wind Lodge. Activities other than the rituals of the secret societies included playing handgame[9] and moccasin game,[10] war dances,[11] feasts,[12] and occasional tribal business meetings. Since the Omahas holistically combine the sacred and secular, such recreational activities also occupy a ritual realm.

The floor plan seems to have been laid out the same in all lodges. The actual as well as ritual entrance was at the eastern quarter. Movement followed a clockwise circle, with the head people seated on the west side of the room. The home crowd sat on the north side of the room, where the heating stove was more likely to be found. Visitors sat along the south side. The singers sat at the center of the room, except for handgames when competing teams provided singers who sat on the north and south side lines.

The combined memories of the Omaha elders identified more dance lodges than were found in the Euro-American record for the period 1890-1930[13] (Figure 2.4). Initial stories focused on lodge locations and the people associated with the societies that used them. Elders seldom concentrated on details of physical structure or recalled specific dates of construction, remodeling, or demolition. The Omaha lodges were remembered in an areal rather than a chronological manner on the landscape; being recalled more by aspects of " who," "where," and "why"—and less by "when."

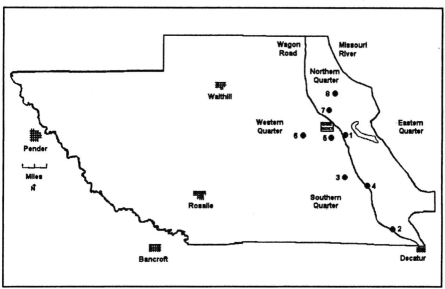

Figure 2.4 Eight Omaha Dance Lodges, Arranged Relative to Macy, Nebraska. 1900-1969. Note reservation boundaries shown after 1882. Source: Composite memories of elders; Conservation and Survey Division aerial photographs, 1938/1940/1949 Series; Nebraska State Historical Society photographs.

The contemporary focus of the reservation landscape is the Omaha Tribal Offices with the arrangement of lodge sites encircling the town of Macy. The eight lodge sites identified by elders are presented here using the Omahas' traditional approach to any ritual place. Beginning on the east side of town, the lodges are discussed in a clockwise order. They are identified by landowner, group name, or prominent member's name. They include the Silas Wood Lodge, Hiram Mitchell Lodge, Peter Blackbird/Orphan Lodge, Warren Davis/Skunk/Little Skunk Lodge, Matthew Tyndall Lodge, Wind/Blackfeet Lodge, Big Crazy/Horse Head Lodge, and the Gilbert Morris/Little Crazy Lodge (Table 2.1). A discussion of lodge location and associated activities is followed by a summary of their architectural features.

Table 2.1 Omaha Dance Lodge Locations and Dates of Existence

Lodge Name	Earliest Date(s)	Latest Date(s)	Location
SILAS WOOD	before 1921	before 1938	SE1/4 of the SW1/4, Section 30, T. 25 N., R. 10 E.
HIRAM MITCHELL	after 1906	before 1930, possibly before 1920	SW1/4 of the NW1/4, Section 27, T. 24 N., R. 10 E.
PETER BLACKBIRD/ ORPHANS	ca. 1920	ca. 1925	NW1/4 of the NW1/4, Section 7, T. 24., R. 10 E.
WARREN DAVIS/ OLD SKUNKS/ YOUNG SKUNKS	ca. 1923	1938-1940	NW1/4 of the SE1/4, Section 8, T. 24. N., R. 10 E.
MATTHEW TYNDALL	before 1920	before 1944	SE1/4 of the SW1/4, Section 25, T. 25 N., R. 9 E.
WIND/ BLACKFEET	before 1930?	1938-1940	NW1/4 of the SE1/4, Section 27, T. 25 N., R. 9 E.
HORSEHEAD/ BIG CRAZY	ca. 1895	1969	NW1/4 of the NE1/4, Section 13, T. 25 N., R. 9 E.
GILBERT MORRIS/ LITTLE CRAZY	before 1930	before 1944	SE1/4 of the NW1/4, Section 24, T. 25 N., R. 9 E.

Sources: Composite memories of Omaha elders; Conservation and Survey Division aerial photographs, 1938/1940/1949 Series; Nebraska State Historical Society photographs; Jerry Maryott Photograph Collection; Steven Standingwater, "People of the Smokey Waters," 9.

EASTERN QUARTER

SILAS WOOD

A lodge was located within the wedge of land at the confluence of the North Blackbird and South Blackbird Creeks, one mile east, and one-quarter mile south of the Omaha Tribal Offices. This southwest one-quarter section appeared upon allotment maps as belonging to Jonathan Parker,

Pede'gahi (Fire Chief).[14] John G. Neihardt, the Nebraska poet laureate, included this lodge in his political satire "A Political Coup at Little Omaha."[15] He described it as "...a large octagonal shack placed in a lonesome valley a mile distant from the Agency." In the story a party of Republican politicians went to the lodge to lobby for votes in an upcoming election. Neihardt only briefly refers to ritual activity and architectural features when he wrote: "As the party neared the lodge, from which the light of the fire within streamed out through the windows into the moon haze, they heard the sound of the drum and the singing that accompanies an Indian feast."[16]

The elders, however, do not recollect Parker as the builder of the lodge and accompanying horse racing track that sat east of Macy. Instead, it is attributed to Silas Wood. Silas Wood's allotment is shown on maps to be the adjoining northwest one-quarter section, located on the north side of North Blackbird Creek.[17] Contemporary common usage has the name spoken and spelled as 'Woods'. Unless otherwise cited this paper maintains the 'Wood' spelling used in allotment documents.

There are several photographs of the area known locally as the "Silas Woods Place." The images vary, with some featuring views of the race track, grandstands, and outdoor dance grounds built by the Wood family.[18] An image from 1921 shows the dance lodge surrounded by a group of tents, tepees, automobiles, and grazing livestock. An American flag on a pole is prominently placed in front of the lodge door[19] (Figure 2.5). A second photograph of the lodge is inscribed "Dance Hall near Macy, Nebr. near Woods Home. 1922."[20]

Figure 2.5 Silas Wood Powwow Grounds, ca. 1921. Photograph by Margaret Koenig. (Courtesy Nebraska State Historical Society, photo no. RG2010:23).

The primary activities attributed to the lodge revolved around the *Xthexe'*, or Mark of Honor Tattoo. A man gained the privilege of having certain tattoos placed upon a female relative by performing war exploits and acts of generosity. This was one of the rituals, mentioned earlier, that Agent Green vigorously opposed among the Otoes. The women who received the tattoos were elevated in status and joined the exclusive *Ho[n]'hewachi*, or Night Blessed Society.[21] Mead reported that the last hereditary tattoo giver died two decades before her 1930 visit, a pretender having taken his place.[22] The allegation was repeated by an elder in 1992.[23] Several elders remembered witnessing the Tattoo Ceremony at this site, although not always in conjunction with the lodge. Women bearing the Mark of Honor Tattoo can be found among the Omahas today. Other activities attributed to the Silas Wood place included the Marble Society dances,[24] moccasin games,[25] peyote church meetings,[26] and feasts.

In the summer of 1906, Eunice Woodhull Stabler witnessed an "Omaha chieftain ceremonial rite" in which the seven hereditary council chiefs gathered in an effort to restore this traditional form of government. The camp on the Wood Powwow ground was described as "a replica of the original setting," that is to say, a replica of the *Hu'thuga* summer buffalo hunt encampment. There was no mention of a dance lodge structure in her account. The tents formed a circle, with two sacred tents in the south center (probably representing the Sacred Pole and the Sacred Buffalo Hide), and one tent at the east entrance to the circle (representing the Sacred Tent of War). Parts of the ceremony were private. Stabler noted the presence of a sacred pipe during parts of the public ceremony. This pipe was carried into four tents, signifying that the occupant of the tent had ascended to his rightful place in the Omaha chieftain circle. Stabler noted in retrospect that the ceremony was being enacted by a passing generation and that it would be the last of its kind.[27]

A Pawnee elder from Oklahoma recalled visiting the lodge in the early 1920s on the occasion of a *Wa'wa[n]*, or, Pipe Dance Ceremony. At least six Pawnee families camped near the building while performing the full-length four-day ritual for the Omahas. They hired two railroad stock cars to transport back to Oklahoma the numerous horses gifted to them by their Omaha hosts.[28]

SOUTHERN QUARTER

HIRAM MITCHELL

The parcel of land upon which the earliest southern lodge stood was originally allotted to Jane Harvey, and subsequently to Elizabeth Harvey.[29] The lodge is remembered as being at the Hiram Mitchell home, the name of the man who resided on the land. The structure stood on the north bank of Wood Creek, six miles south and three and one-half miles east of the

Omaha Tribal Offices. The original allotment home, recently remodeled, still stands to the east of the lodge site. This is the only lodge site in Burt County, Nebraska. There was no particular lodge name or group name given to the structure. It was later moved to at least two other locations before it was abandoned.

Hiram Mitchell is remembered as a prominent member of the early peyote church.[30] This synthesis of Christian and traditional native religions arrived on the nearby Winnebago reservation in 1897 and was active among the Omaha by 1906. Ninety-seven Omahas were recorded as members of the Mescal Society in 1912, with some having been already active for five years. Omahas petitioned the federal government for permission to practice peyotism in 1915 and 1916. The petition included personal statements from Peter Blackbird, Sam Gilpin, Thomas Walker, and Simon Hallowell. All of these men were residents in the area surrounding the lodge. Hiram Mitchell wrote that he was "of the first who used the peyote root (about eight years ago)."[31]

It is unclear when the lodge was built at the Mitchell place. Three elders confirmed that the peyote society held church services in a circular lodge at that place.[32] One elder described the building as a "smaller lodge."[33] The ground-level hearth and a half-moon altar were permanently laid out in concrete on the floor of the lodge (Figure 2.6). For a time, the religious group seemed to be the main users of the building. The elders recalled a displacement by a second group whose purpose was social, sacred, or some combination of the two.[34] Reports of Marble Society dancing and handgames being played in the lodge suggest a blend of new uses.[35] There was no accounting for the disposition of the concrete hearth and altar during this transition. Ultimately, the lodge was moved by the new group to

Figure 2.6 Peyote Religion Cement Fireplace, 1907. Photograph by Melvin Gilmore (Courtesy Nebraska State Historical Society, photo no. 1394, 2–1).

the Peter Blackbird home in the early 1920s. It is not known to what degree the lodge was dismantled and how much, if anything, was salvaged for reuse.

PETER BLACKBIRD/ORPHAN

The Peter Blackbird home has been tentatively identified by an elder as being on the Walter Blackbird allotment.[36] The lodge site occupied a flat clearing of land on the west bank of South Blackbird Creek, two and one-half miles south, and three-quarters of a mile east of the Omaha Tribal Offices. It was due west of the Bud King farmhouse. The lodge was rebuilt and became known as the *Waho^n' thi^{n}ge*, Orphan Lodge. The origin and significance of the name is undetermined. The Orphans played shinny[37] game against other groups on a nearby hay field. Participants in the *I^n'kugthi^n athi^n*, Pebble or Marble Society Dance, were associated with this lodge, suggesting a mixture of sacred and secular activities.

No description of the physical structure has been recorded beyond the standard dance lodge form already offered. One elder remembered the Orphan Lodge alongside Blackbird Creek between 1920-1925.[38] Another elder recalled a "homemade" lodge being full of mud, suggesting intermittent maintenance.[39] There was speculation that the land was lost due to foreclosure and the lodge sold to the Little Skunk organization.[40] In any event, the Orphan group declined in the early 1920s, and the lodge was moved once again. It is unclear how it was dismantled, or if materials were salvaged, before it reappeared two miles down the road and across the creek at the Warren Davis home.

WARREN DAVIS/SKUNK/LITTLE SKUNK

The location of this lodge was on land first allotted to James Dixon, which subsequently became the Daniel Porter Blackbird allotment, and then the Walter Edwards allotment.[41] Warner or Warren Davis, husband of Lizzie Edwards, gave his name to this site. The land is three and one-quarter miles south, and two miles east of the Omaha Tribal Offices. It is undoubtedly the "Badger Lodge" referenced by Margaret Mead in 1930.[42] Of all the Omaha lodges, this southern example has the most complex history.

The essence of the mystery is how this lodge occupied two other sites before coming to rest at the Warren Davis place. Despite being utilized by different social or religious groups at each of these sites, this particular lodge remains in memory as a single structure. Several elders recalled the lodge coming, somehow, from the Peter Blackbird home located two miles to the northwest. The oldest resource elder who was born and raised in this region of the reservation provided a complete narrative of the multiple locations. In this version, the first lodge was built at the Hiram Mitchell home along Wood Creek. From there it was moved to the Peter Blackbird home on the west bank of South Blackbird Creek, and later came to rest at the Warren Davis home.[43]

This final manifestation of the traveling dance lodge is not without conflicting interpretations. A resident of the southern reservation area recalls the *Mon'ga in'sh'age*, Old Skunk Lodge, being built at the Warren Davis place ca.1923.[44] Of the numerous elders offering information about this lodge, nearly one-half suggested it belonged to the Old Skunk group, claiming that the *Mon'ga zhin'ga*, Little (or Young) Skunks used private homes for their activities. The balance of the elders staunchly attributed the lodge to the Young Skunks. Both sides concurred that the Young Skunks were a branch from the Old Skunks.[45] The lodge was the site of many dances, handgames, feasts, and shinny games. It is possible that at least one performance of the *Wa'wan*, or Pipe Dance Ceremony, was performed at the Old Skunk Lodge.[46]

MATTHEW TYNDALL

The parcel of land upon which another lodge stood was originally allotted to Matthew Tyndall, and ownership remained unchanged through subsequent allotments.[47] The lodge sat upon a flat clearing one-half mile south, and one-quarter mile west of the Omaha Tribal Offices. An unidentified photograph taken near 1920 has been attributed to this site (Figure 2.7).[48] It shows a group of people seated in the grass in front of a lodge, surrounded by horses, wagons, and automobiles. A brick chimney is visible passing through the cupola windows and protruding from the top.[49] What

Figure 2.7 Matthew Tyndall Lodge(?), ca. 1920. (Courtesy Jerry Maryott, Decatur, Nebraska)

activities took place in the Matthew Tyndall lodge have yet to be determined. One elder referred to this place as the "Chiefs' Lodge" because of its association with, and use by, members of the *We' zhi^nshte* (Elk) Clan - relatives of the prominent nineteenth century leader Big Elk.[50]

WESTERN QUARTER

WIND/BLACKFEET

A lodge was on land first allotted to Eunice Wood, which subsequently was allotted to Sarah Webster.[51] The building occupied the extreme northwest corner of the tract. A portion of an unnamed stream that flows into North Blackbird Creek and the western edge of the clearing fell within the Henry Matthews allotment.[52] The site is two miles west of the Omaha Tribal Offices. *Tade' ti*, or, Wind Lodge, is one of three names most consistently applied to this structure. A group by the same name used the lodge. A second local group called *Çi'çabe*, Blackfeet, also used the lodge and their name is often attached to the structure. A third appellation is the Harry Lyon's Lodge, named for the man who lived due north of the structure. A single elder called the building the Horseshoe Lodge.[53] While not readily obvious to a casual observer standing on the site, a distinctive horseshoe bend in the surrounding creek becomes apparent from the vantage point of a rise of land north of the lodge. This structure was most likely the "Rainbow" lodge noted by Mead in 1930.[54]

Activities at the Wind Lodge included a range of sacred and secular dances, feasts, moccasin games, and handgames. A reference to "people with bundles" using the lodge suggested the activities of the Shell Society or Pebble Society, since members of both organizations kept their ritual paraphernalia stored inside bundles, bags, or trunks.[55] The Wind Lodge was the location of the humorous Christmas tree fire.[56] Directly west of the lodge, across the creek on the Henry Matthews allotment, was the site of an accompanying outdoor dance grounds. Social groups used the side hill and ridge top as camping and dance grounds This practice continued after the Wind Lodge was dismantled. The popularity of the location was evidenced by the effort expended to bring in a steam merry-go-round to entertain week-long encampments. War dancers would travel from as far away as Decatur to participate in the all-night festivities.[57] A lack of good quality water and sanitation in the sweltering summer heat seemed to result in at least one death annually during the site's use.[58]

NORTHERN QUARTER

BIG CRAZY/HORSE HEAD

The Horse Head Lodge, located two and one-half miles north of the

Omaha Tribal Offices, and named for the nearby Horse Head Creek, is the most publicly known structure. It was the lodge identified by Margaret Mead as the "Buffalo Lodge."[59] It stood on the Eli S. Parker, *Gthedo^n no^{n}zhi^n* (Standing Hawk) allotment.[60] James Owen Dorsey placed Standing Hawk with the nearby village of *Win-dja'-ge*.[61] Standing Hawk's great granddaughter, now an elder in her own right, suggested that the original lodge was built in her great grandfather's time.[62] Her reminiscence is supported by a postscript in an undated personal letter, possibly written in April 1895, by Edward Farley to Francis La Flesche. In it, Farley notes that "Noah [Leaming, the brother-in-law of both Farley and La Flesche] was out a day or so ago with eight or ten teams [of horses] to get lumber to build a round dancing house, 60 feet across, not far from his home."[63] Noah and his wife Lucy La Flesche reportedly occupied a house due north of the Parker allotment for a time.

The Horse Head Lodge was remodeled and used sporadically over the years, reflecting the shifting resources and interests of the social organizations. Those renovations are apparent in the few surviving photographs of the lodge. The Sheldon photograph of 1905 showed a newly laid shake shingle roof. The shingles over the northern gable window had yet to be trimmed.[64] A similar view in 1912, titled "Standing Hawk Lodge," featured a stove pipe protruding through the northern gable roof.[65]

Sho^n'ge pa, or, "Horse Head," is generally accepted as the name for the structure. The main organization that used the lodge was given the designation *Gtho^{n}thi^n to^{n}ga*, "Big Crazies," in an often-repeated story. One version recounts how a man and his wife drove to an activity at the lodge in a lumber wagon with a matched pair of horses. The man got so excited during the event that he spontaneously gave away one of the horses from his matched team. When the activity was concluded and the participants departed for home, the man and his wife were left stranded, having but a single horse that was unable to pull their heavy wagon. The laughter and cries of "*gtho^{n}thi^n to^{n}ga*" (big crazy) filled the nighttime air. The humorous name came to be applied to the whole organization.[66] Later efforts to re-assert the "Horse Head" name to the group never completely succeeded.

Sacred dances were occasionally held at the Horse Head Lodge. Handgames were played year round. The *Hethu'shka zhi^{n}ga* (Little Warriors) held war dances, with feasts and giveaways marking any special occasion. Younger lodge members formed a shinny team to play against other social groups. Euro-American holidays such as Thanksgiving and Halloween were celebrated at the Horse Head Lodge with dances and handgames. Pranksters at the Halloween activities would often switch the draft horses of participants in the lodge. Sleepy revelers would load up their wagons in the dark after the dance and give the horses a free rein to go home, only to find themselves pulling into someone else's barn.[67]

GILBERT MORRIS/LITTLE CRAZY

The *Gtho^{n}thi^n zhi^{n}ga*, "Little Crazy" Lodge was located one mile north of the Omaha Tribal Offices. The land was first allotted to Simon Morris and later became the Gilbert Morris allotment.[68] Nestled among the trees, it was built south of the family home sometime before 1930. Identified by Margaret Mead as the "Little Deer Lodge," an offshoot of the "Buffalo Lodge,"[69] the name "Little Crazy" is indicative of this offspring relationship to the older "Big Crazy" organization. More commonly referred to as the Gilbert Morris Lodge, it drew a uniform response of being the site of the *xube wachi'gaxe*, the sacred dances. Many elders recalled attending Shell Society and Pebble Society dances as very young children. Their descriptions of events consistently focused upon the powerful, frightening, and strict nature of the dances.[70] Most remembered these two societies as the exclusive users of the lodge, while some others suggested that the Little Warriors used the place for war dances.[71]

Why did these eight wooden dance lodges come into existence? Most elders responded, "They were for the *xube wachigaxe* (sacred people dance)." A single elder suggested the federal government built the lodges as an expedient remedy for communal housing.[72] However, the broad catalog of activities held at each lodge confirms that the structures were clearly serving as an important gathering place for secular and sacred events. The versatility of the structure's space answered the needs of a wide range of users. The spirit of communal sharing permitted groups and individuals access to lodge facilities to which they did not necessarily belong.

The Shell and Pebble Societies reportedly used most of the lodges, although they may not have constructed or exercised ownership at all of these locations. A sacred society's appellation of "secret" referred to the content of the rituals and did not impact where meetings took place, as none of the lodges were hidden on the landscape nor were the dates of activities concealed from the community.[73] Considering the location of roads during this period, all of the lodges were accessible by foot, saddle horse, wagon, and later, automobile. Easy physical access, nearby firewood, and dependable water made lodges ideal for extended, sometimes week-long, gatherings.

It is the diversity of usage that is the most salient feature of the lodges. All of the lodges which hosted the Shell and/or Pebble Society activities were also the sites for the social handgame and/or moccasin game. Some of the social activities were sponsored by secret societies, while others were sponsored by social groups or individuals. Specialized activities, such as the Mark of Honor Tattoo and Peyote Church, were only reported for lodges owned by persons with socially recognized rights to conduct such ceremonies. Feasts and giveaways were a relatively common occurrence in most lodges, while hosting of the more expensive Pipe Dance was a rare event.

Euro-American holiday observances were not widely reported, being restricted to the Wind Lodge and Big Crazy Lodge. Their proximity to the Agency and Presbyterian Mission, respectively, may reflect an expression of heightened acculturation. However, it is more likely that the full range of Omaha traditional social activities were held on Euro-American holidays at all lodges. This proposal is based upon several suppositions. Holiday (and weekend) activities, versus mid-week events, would not draw undue complaints from local Indian agents or school officials. With the increase of wage labor and rigidly scheduled relief program work after 1930, holidays would be one of the few days available for social activities. By the 1940s, holiday scheduling would accommodate participation from relatives working off-reservation. Finally, many of the social activities reported for lodges were as often remembered by *who* sponsored the event, as by the date of their occurrence. Further inquiry may uncover additional connections between reported activities and their dates of occurrence relative to Euro-American holidays. It may be that certain lodge groups routinely organized activities on particular holidays, involved other lodge groups as their invited guests, and thus effectively monopolized and localized the holiday. Such a practice was common in the 1960s and 1970s with the descendants of the Horse Head Lodge "traditionally" hosting a Christmas activity at the Macy community building.

The elders offered descriptions of various architectural features for several lodges as they appeared since the late 1930s.[74] They recalled that the societies or social groups drew upon the knowledge and skills of their own members to build the lodges. Many Omaha men had been trained as carpenters by Indian agents in order to construct the agency buildings and allotment homes. These talents were harnessed in the creation of the dance lodges as evidenced by the similarity of architectural details shared by the lodges and nearby homes. Appearing superficially identical, each dance lodge had distinctive features. The number of side walls varied, as did window sizes and details, the presence of a cupola, and the complexity of the roof. Beginning again in the east, the following structures will be examined in a clockwise order: the Silas Wood Lodge, Warren Davis/Skunk/Little Skunk Lodge, Matthew Tyndall Lodge, Wind/Blackfeet Lodge, Big Crazy/Horse Head Lodge, and the Gilbert Morris/Little Crazy Lodge.

EASTERN QUARTER

SILAS WOOD

A 1922 photograph provides an excellent view of the exterior features of the lodge (Figure 2.8).[75] The eight-sided outer walls were covered with clapboard siding. Simple square windows were placed in alternating walls. A steeply pitched shake shingle roof was topped by a small cupola with tar paper and wood covered windows. A metal stove pipe protruded from the cupola roof, suggesting some type of stove being used. A ring of six or eight posts reportedly supported the roof, with an open fire pit in the center of the floor.[76] A stout native timber flagpole stood to the east of the door.

Figure 2.8 Silas Wood Dance Lodge, 1922. Photograph by Nathaniel Lee Dewell. (Courtesy Nebraska State Historical Society, photo no. RG3882:54–40).

SOUTHERN QUARTER

WARREN DAVIS/SKUNK/LITTLE SKUNK

Descriptions of the Skunk Lodge follow the standard form already defined. Overall size was said to be larger than the Horse Head Lodge, but the roof was not as steep. The cedar shake roof did not have a cupola. Those elders that maintained the absence of windows in other lodges confirmed the same condition for this structure. The single center pole may have had braces attached to the rafters.[77] Homemade plank and post benches formed a single ring along the inside of the wall. Tables were provided along the north wall for holding food. A wood heater and stove pipe sat inside the door on the north side. Cooking was done outside. Light was provided by kerosene lanterns.

MATTHEW TYNDALL

The c.1920 photograph from the Maryott collection of this lodge includes a view of the front door, side walls with small window, shake shingle roof, and a square cupola (Figure 2.7). The exterior walls appear newly painted or whitewashed. From the photograph, it appears that the lodge had twelve wall sections. The brick chimney, already noted, is visible passing through the cupola windows and protruding from the top.[78]

A ca.1930s photograph by Otto Wilson has been identified as the Horse Head Lodge (Figure 2.9) The photographer noted that the lodge had been "destroyed by fire."[79] Oral histories do not support such an event related to the Horse Head Lodge, but do compare with stories about the demise of the Gilbert Morris Lodge. No ground level photographs of the Gilbert Morris Lodge are available for comparison. A re-examination of the Wilson photograph tentatively suggests that it may be another view of the Matthew Tyndall lodge. This attribution is based upon the similarities in architectural features with the Maryott photograph including exterior wall covering, cupola orientation and chimney height, window size and type, distinctive roof ridge lines, protruding door posts, and the overall height of the side walls.

Figure 2.9 Omaha Dance Lodge, ca. 1930s. Mabel Campbell Wilson and an unidentified Harlan boy. Photograph by Otto Wilson. Wilson, *Camera Man and Picture Woman*, 27 (Courtesy of Ralph Wilson).

WESTERN QUARTER

WIND/BLACKFEET

Descendants of the Wind Lodge/Blackfeet Lodge groups provided information about its architectural features. The circular roof was supported by
a single native timber post. The stove sat nearby on the dirt floor, the metal
stove pipe going straight up through the roof. There were the usual differences of opinion about the existence of windows. Pump-up gasoline
lanterns that periodically went dim were used. The interior was remembered as dark.[80] Removable homemade plank benches were used in later
years. The lodge contained a stuffed eagle that was later removed to
Lincoln, Nebraska.[81] Water came from a spring along the surrounding
creek. A well was also dug for the lodge. A rectangular cement stock tank
was provided for the horses.

NORTHERN QUARTER

BIG CRAZY/Horse HEAD

The elders remember several versions of the physical structure. There was
a uniformity of agreement about the lodge being circular, with a packed
earth floor and the doorway facing the east. The side walls were unfin-
ished, with the upright 2 x 4 lumber visible on the inside. The number of
panels making up the exterior wall seems to vary between nine and twelve.
Seating was on the floor, with a single ring of homemade plank-and-post
benches being added later. Most elders recalled a single central post next to
the brick chimney. Others remembered a ring of four or more posts, either
placed near the chimney or somewhere between the chimney and the sidewalls.[82] In later years, probably when the chimney was added, a cupola
topped the roof.[83]

The existence of windows is uncertain. The photographs aside, about
one half of the elders did not recall windows in the Horse Head Lodge. The
lack of memory about this particular feature could be attributed to several
factors. The young age of the elder at the time; the fact that windows were
covered after dusk, for sacred dances, and while eating; or the strong
Omaha taboo against looking in windows from the outside. Light was provided by pump-up gas lanterns and kerosene "horse barn" lanterns. Heat
was furnished by a round barrel stove located to the right of the door.
Cooking was done outside, with the food being placed on a table along the
inside wall.

GILBERT MORRIS/LITTLE CRAZY

The physical structure was remembered as being quite similar to the

Horse Head Lodge. The amount of natural shade at the site was emphasized. There were the usual differences of memories about particular features. A chimney and one or more posts were located in the center of the
packed-earth floor. The stove was described as being without legs and able
to accommodate a soup cauldron sitting in the center. Windows were not
remembered clearly. A cupola adorned the roof.

All of the dance lodges blended innovative new materials with traditional technologies. The use of milled lumber, shake shingles, glass windows, brick chimneys, and galvanized metal ridge caps was combined with
earth lodge construction techniques. An inspection of one lodge used by the
Shell Society revealed the timber posts at the exterior walls were not significantly bearing the roof load. They seemed to act only as stabilizers
against horizontal movement.[84] By extrapolation, the roof load must have
been born by the single or multiple central posts in the same manner that
earth lodges were designed.

Including windows in a secret society structure that so closely emulated
the windowless earth lodge was another innovation. It was a common
sense adaptation of Euro-American architecture that helped to illuminate
the interior of the lodge. Nonetheless, windows and mirrors were controlled by several cultural taboos. Their presence seemed to have been actually, or ritually, ignored as evidenced by the elders' lack of memory of them.

Were these lodges preserving Omaha culture and an expression of resistance, or were they evidence of cultural innovation and change? In effect,
the lodges represented both preservation and innovation. They were something old - they were something new. The activities held at these sites were
the most visible evidence of this duality. A traditional Pebble Society secret
meeting, a prayer service of the introduced Peyote Church, and a
handgame held on Christmas Day, illustrate the range of the lodge as cultural protector and cultural innovator.

Lodge membership rested upon the neighborhood, and arguably grew
out of the isolation created by dispersal from villages onto allotments.
Small groups would form around the lodge, exist for a short time, then dis-
solve.[85] Elders recalled that members of a group would donate labor, lumber, and personal sawmills to build their own lodge.[86] Lodges were placed
on the lands of a group member. There is no evidence that any lodge was
built, owned, or controlled by the tribal corporate body, or any non-
Omaha entity. This supports the notion of a completely neighborhood-
based organization. Therefore, looking at the nature of neighborhoods on
the Omaha reservation might give some clues about the creation of dance
lodges.

Fewer Omahas resided on western allotments after 1910. As allotments
were sold in the 1890s, most being partial holdings in the west, many
Omahas returned to the vicinity of the three eastern villages where they

maintained the balance of their lands. The allotment process did not result then in the eradication of all things "Indian" as desired by the reformers. Public expressions of patrilocal residence, such as the *Hu'thuga* arrangement of the buffalo hunt, were reduced to occasional encampments at summer dances. The matrilocal residence pattern remained strong and pervasive, with many husbands continuing the practice of living with the wife's family and providing service to the father-in-Law.[87] Numerous Omahas resumed the extended matrilocal family groups of traditional village life.[88]

The division into three villages in 1855 has been characterized as a radical innovation indicating tribal schism. By 1910 the new generation born on the isolated allotments looked to the three villages as "traditional" points of origin. Their return to matrilocal residences of large household clusters near the old village sites allowed for the use of traditional behavior patterns to deal with growing social and economic problems.[89] A major element in Omaha history on the Plains has been the struggle to maintain tribal unity in the face of external forces. The migration back to the sacred and ancestral sites near the Missouri River bluffs could be seen as a repeat of the move made in 1855. Faced with the prospects of relocation to Indian Territory in the nineteenth century, the Omahas chose to take their reservation on familiar Nebraska terrain. Fifty years later, the traumas of allotment, isolation, forced assimilation, and poverty caused the people to gather again along the Missouri River. However, the communal village-type reunification could not be achieved under the divisive nature of the surviving allotment system. The result was a pattern of emerging kin-related neighborhoods scattered in a band along the agency wagon road from Horse Head Creek in the north to Wood Creek in the south.

All of the dance lodges arose in the eastern one-third of the reservation, appearing at, or after, the turn of the century. It was during this period that the government's nineteenth century theoretical and religiously oriented dream of Christian reformers gave way to pragmatic, practical approaches of businesslike management. The allotment process had turned a few tribal units into a nightmare of thousands of individual wards of the government. Key words in the new century were "self-support" and "self-reliance." Meanwhile, the Indian Service branch of the federal government came to dominate every aspect of Omaha life.[90]

Pressures continued for assimilation. Economic, political, religious, and social controls forced Omaha traditions further underground. While the clan system appeared on the decline, and with it any social cohesion its arrangements offered, many of the activities in the lodges centered upon the societies. Societies cut across clan lines, had a tendency to be endogamous, and created firm interlocking groups that served to check any trend toward disruption.[91] Since most of the societies were organized and dominated by men, it can be said that the societies came to replace the patrilineal clans in the maintenance of social and cultural cohesion. It may be that this male domination of the societies nullified any organizational patterns imposed by the practice of matrilocal residence. Forming tighter groups, the societies were able to mobilize resources for maintenance of their rituals. Daily farm chores and difficulty in travel meant that lodge members generally lived in the surrounding countryside. Groups were composed of blood or marriage-related individuals from multiple clans. Faced with limited floor space in the square-walled, multi-partitioned allotment homes, an innovation was the use of a structure other than a society member's personal dwelling for meetings. The result was a change in ownership or control patterns. Some of the new dance lodges were owned or controlled by the society, unlike the earlier family earth lodges which were owned by one or two individuals.

There was a division within at least one social club upon gender lines. Descriptions of the Little Skunk organization in the southern reservation area refer to men and women gathering in separate groups. The men might congregate inside of the lodge while the women sat under the shade trees outdoors. Each gender group would discuss club business prior to a collective meeting. Ideas or suggestions generated in either group would often be supported by the second group.[92] While only reported for this single organization of the era, gender-divided socialization was not uncommon. Male-only groups such as the *Hethu'shka* (Warrior) Society, were gender-specific in a formal sense. Informally, men and women would travel to visit same-sex kin, while children were encouraged to interact with same-sex playmates.[93]

Omaha dance lodges were constructed at the turn of the century as a continuation of the traditional need for ritual space. Previously centered in the *Hu'thuga*, earth lodge, and tepee, this space was now located in, and supported by kin-based neighborhoods. Being built and maintained through private funds meant the lodges did not draw any fiscal notice from the Indian agent. The space fulfilled the ritual requirements found in the earlier earth lodge form.[94] The secretive nature of the more sacred dances protected the societies from outside interference. Thus, the milled wood structure provided appropriate camouflage for Omahas to continue a wide range of cultural activities. The societies survived internal and external pressures that incapacitated or destroyed other tribal institutions. The *xube wachigaxe* (sacred people dance) and social activities sponsored by kin-based, neighborhood-oriented societies served to unify Omahas in the face of assimilation forces.

The lodges also included innovative construction techniques, ownership patterns, and aspects of use. A structure such as this would have been a feature in white communities of that era. The idea of a large building for Euro-American social activities may have been acceptable to the non-Omaha powers, interpreted as a move towards acculturation into white society. The Omaha celebration of Euro-American holidays with dances and parties meant the lodges were an avenue towards selective acculturation, and may have been an aspect of emulation of Euro-American culture.

While the Omahas were receiving new cultural ideas, they were also transmitting aspects of their culture abroad. A principal dance form of the Plains powwow is the *Hethu'shka* (War Dance). There is a large body of scholarly literature devoted to the origins and variations of this dance.[95] The Omahas are generally acknowledged by other tribes as the originators of this dance. This legacy is preserved by the practice of many Plains tribes referring to their war dance as the "Omaha" dance. The *Hethu'shka* Society was an important group using several dance lodges. There seems to be evidence of the export of the dance lodge structure along with the *Hethu'shka* dance. A military map of the 1890 massacre at Wounded Knee, South Dakota, features a six-sided structure north of the battle site marked as "The Omaha."[96] In 1891, residents of the Pine Ridge Reservation in South Dakota traveled to Chadron, Nebraska to "purchase lumber for the erection of a large powwow house in which to hold Omaha dances."[97] The question of whether the lodges in other native communities owe their origins to the Omaha remains an intriguing area of inquiry for a broader comparative study.

Dance lodges flourished on the Omaha landscape from the late 1890s through the late1930s. Why did the secret societies and the lodges they support decline and disappear by the mid-1940s? Did the preservation of traditional customs and the resistance to assimilation collapse? Was the unifying function of the societies replaced in some manner? These questions will be explored during the period of 1930-1960, even though the frequent response to queries about Omaha tradition and ritual for this era was a frustrating "*Itha paho^n mo^{n}zhi^n*, I had not asked about it."

NOTES

1. Adapted from a story presented by Elder QQQ, summer 1992.

2. Nebraska State Historical Society, Lincoln, Nebraska. Photograph No. RG2039:15. Photograph by Addison E. Sheldon.

3. Fletcher and La Flesche, *The Omaha Tribe*, 516.

4. Ibid., 516–519.

5. Ibid., 565–581.

6. Mead, *Changing Culture*, xiii.

7. Ibid., 34.

8. For the purposes of maintaining anonymity for the elder informants regarding specific statements, each was assigned an arbitrary 2-letter or 3-letter code. Those elders that gave permission to be cited for their participation are credited in the list at the end of the paper. The use of personal names of deceased individuals is frowned upon in contemporary Omaha society. Speaking about such individuals during formal interviews and casual conversations usually relied upon kinship terms, both biological and otherwise. Out of respect for this cultural practice, few personal names are included in the text.

9. Elders suggest that the handgame, $I^n{}'uti^n$ (striking the stone), was probably introduced to the Omaha by the Otoe. The contemporary interpretation of this popular guessing game contains many ritual procedures and admonitions, placing it in a sacred realm. One team attempts to guess the location of two stones hidden in the hands of two opponents. Points are lost due to wrong guesses. Penalties are extracted from the losing team. Game sponsors will provide a wager or prize for the winning team. Games are interspersed with social dances and humorous antics. Howard, *The Ponca Tribe*, 128–129, records the Ponca receiving their version of the handgame from the Pawnee.

10. Moccasin game, $Hi^nbe\ uti^n$ (striking the moccasin), [or maybe $Hi^nbe\ ugtha$ (calling the moccasin?)], was popular in the first half of the century. No elder could recall a recent game on the Omaha reservation, although the neighboring Winnebago continue to play. The game involved two teams facing each other across a blanket spread on the ground. A small object was secreted inside a receptacle, generally a moccasin. Each side took turns trying to guess in which of the four moccasins the object was hidden. Bystanders and players sang songs and made remarks as a strategy to unnerve the person with the stone, thus revealing where the object was hidden through some expression or gesture. See Dorsey, *Omaha Sociology*, 339.

11. The war dance of the late nineteenth century was performed by members of the *Hethu'shka* Society, a warrior's social organization. Membership was originally restricted to combat veterans, and eligibility to wear the distinctive feathered regalia strictly regulated. The *Hethu'shka zhi''ga*, Little Warrior Society, formed in the twentieth century. Membership was not restricted to veterans, and the dance spread outside of the confines of the original society. See Fletcher and La Flesche, 441–442, 459–480.

12. Feasts were sponsored by individuals, families, and groups as a personal sacrifice that validated or commemorated an event. Occasions for a feast could include such events as a birthday, anniversary, funeral or memorial, to honor visiting guests, or to acknowledge children returning or departing for school. Material goods were usually given to visitors at a feast. All who attended provided their own eating utensils, and left-over food was distributed to the needy. This practice continues today.
13. Of the 50-plus elders interviewed, no single individual could recall the location, use, and history of all of the dance lodges on the Omaha reservation. From their stories and directions there were more than the "four" lodges identified by Mead. Elders offered descriptions of the building sites, architectural features, organizations that used the lodges, and the diverse range of activities. Divergent or conflicting data was not arbitrarily discounted.

14. Painter, "Omaha Indian Allotments, 1871," 14; Fletcher, "Omaha Indian Allotments, 1882–1883," 94; Fletcher and La Flesche, *The Omaha Tribe*, 643–654.

15. John G. Neihardt, A Political Coup at Little Omaha, *IN* The Ancient Memory and Other Stories, edited by Hilda Neihardt Petri. Lincoln: University of Nebraska Press, 1991. 51–69.

16. Ibid., 61.

17. Fletcher, "Omaha Indian Allotments, 1882–1883," 194; Fletcher and La Flesche, *The Omaha Tribe*, 643–654.

18.Other photographs of the Silas Wood homestead include Photograph No. RG1289:11–3, Nebraska State Historical Society, Lincoln, Nebraska. Inscribed "On Omaha Agency. Decater (sic), Neb.", it features a close-up view of the ticket office and entrance to the race track, with the wooden archway inscribed "Omaha Indian Race~Track Association." A Photograph by Nathaniel Lee Dewell, Photograph No. RG3882:54–39, Nebraska State Historical Society. Entitled "Wood Family On Way To Powwow at Macy, Nebraska, September 1922", it shows members of the Wood family in a horse-drawn wagon posed in front of the dance lodge.

19. Photograph No. RG2010:23. Nebraska State Historical Society, Lincoln, Nebraska. Photograph by Margaret Koenig. The front of the image is inscribed

"Silas Woods Powwow grounds—1 mile east of Macy— Above—last Tatoe (sic) ceremony—Woods place." An inscription on the back of the photograph may not pertain to the image. It is a list of days and dates (without year), and a notation about "work day" and "rain day." The combination of days and dates suggest the year to be 1921.

20. Nebraska State Historical Society, Lincoln, Nebraska. Photograph No. RG3882:54–40. Photograph by Nathaniel Lee Dewell. Further inscription on the back of the photograph reads "Built by Silas Wood, Lodge Hall with no name."

21. Fletcher and La Flesche, *The Omaha Tribe*, 500–509; For a contemporary summary and interpretation of The Mark of Honor, see Ridington and Hastings, *Blessing for a Long Time.*

22. Mead, *Changing Culture*, 135–136.

23. Elder MMM, summer 1992.

24. Elder GG, summer 1992.

25. Elder ZZ, summer 1992.

26. Elder UU, summer 1992.

27. Stephen Cobb, et al., *La-ta-we-sah (Woman of the Bird clan)*, 22–3.

28. Elder UUU, autumn 1993. Similarities in Pipe Dance ceremonies were shared between the Pawnee and Omaha. Reasons for hosting the dance varied. The Omaha ritual emphasized establishing and maintaining peace through the creation of ceremonial kinships; Fletcher and La Flesche, *The Omaha Tribe*, 379.

29. Painter, "Omaha Indian Allotments, 1871," 5; Fletcher, "Omaha Indian Allotments, 1882–1883," 60; Fletcher and La Flesche, *The Omaha Tribe*, 643–654.

30. Elder LL, summer 1992.

31. Omer C. Stewart, *Peyote Religion: A History* (Norman: University of Oklahoma Press, 1987), 162–164.

32. Elders VV, UU, and LL, summer 1992.

33. Elder UU, summer 1992.

34. Elders VV, LL, summer 1992.

35. Elder LL, summer 1992.

36. Elders LL, UU, summer 1992; Painter, "Omaha Indian Allotments, 1871," 1; Fletcher, "Omaha Indian Allotments, 1882–1883," 16; Fletcher and La Flesche, *The Omaha Tribe*, 643–654.

37. A ceremonial ball game called *tabe'gaçi* was played by young men of the two major divisions of the *Hu'thuga*. Similar to field hockey, the two teams were armed with crooked-ended sticks with which to drive a ball between the opponent's goal posts. It was the duty of a member of the *Tade'ata*, or Wind Clan, to start the ball. The game is said to have had cosmic significance. Elders in 1992 referred to the game by the Omaha name or the English term "shinny." Social groups associated with the lodges played against each other. The Wind Clan prerogative was observed during the spring and summer tournament games when team members were predetermined. Casual games among young men in which the teams were chosen on the spot did not follow the Wind Clan restriction. Shinny games were discontinued in the 1940s(?) after a player suffered a broken leg; Fletcher and La Flesche, *The Omaha Tribe*, 197–198, 365–366.

38. Elder UU, summer 1992.

39. Elder EE, summer 1992.

40. Elder UU, summer 1992.

41. Painter, "Omaha Indian Allotments, 1871," 2; Fletcher, "Omaha Indian Allotments, 1882–1883," 19; Fletcher and La Flesche, *The Omaha Tribe*, 643–654.

42. Mead, *Changing Culture*, 34.

43. Elder LL, summer 1992.

44. Elder YY, summer 1992.

45. The term *zhi^nga* referred to a diminutive relationship similar to that between a clan and its subordinate subclans; Fletcher and La Flesche, *The Omaha Tribe*, 136–137.

46. Elder ZZ, summer 1992.

47. Painter, "Omaha Indian Allotments, 1871," 18; Fletcher, "Omaha Indian Allotments, 1882–1883," 155; Fletcher and La Flesche, *The Omaha Tribe*, 643–654.

48. Jerry Maryott Collection photograph on loan to the Nebraska State Historical Society, Lincoln, Nebraska. Jerry Maryott, Decatur, Nebraska.

49. Elder JJJ, summer 1992. This distinctive feature caused the photograph to be originally credited to the Horse Head Lodge. Further scrutiny of the background scenery, together with memories about the favorite sites visited by the photographer supported the Matthew Tyndall attribution.

50. Elder ZA, winter 1999.

51. Painter, "Omaha Indian Allotments, 1871," 18; Fletcher, "Omaha Indian Allotments, 1882–1883," 28; Fletcher, p. 28; Fletcher and La Flesche, *The Omaha Tribe*, 643–654.

52. Painter, "Omaha Indian Allotments, 1871," 18; Fletcher," Omaha Indian Allotments, 1882–1883," 158; Fletcher and La Flesche, *The Omaha Tribe*, 643–654.

53. Elder SS, summer 1992.

54. The third of four lodges reported by Mead was identified as "the Rainbow, within walking distance southwest of Radner (Macy)" (Mead, *Changing Culture*, 34). The early twentieth century core residential and commercial area of Macy was located along the creek that runs diagonally across the NW 1/4 of Section 25, T. 25 N., R. 9 E. The Wind Lodge would have been roughly southwest of Macy's core at the time of Mead's 1930 visit. Sometime prior to World War II several religious, commercial, and residential buildings were relocated toward the southeast edge of town to escape the seasonally muddy conditions near the creek. For this reason McEvoy's 1963 thesis on reservation settlement patterns placed the "Rainbow" lodge site due west of Macy (McEvoy, "Reservation Settlement Patterns," 35–38). Given that the Wind Lodge and Matthew Tyndall Lodge were both clearly present during Mead's visit, but only the former was recorded, it is likely that the Matthew Tyndall Lodge had already fallen into disrepair, was being used by livestock, or was already gone (Elder JJJ, summer 1992).

55. Elder GGG, summer 1992.

56 Elder QQQ, summer 1992.

57. Elder YY, summer 1992.

58. Elder JJJ, summer 1992.

59. Mead, *Changing Culture*, 34.

60. Painter, "Omaha Indian Allotments, 1871," 16; Fletcher, "Omaha Indian Allotments, 1882–1883," 133; Fletcher and La Flesche, *The Omaha Tribe*, 643–654.

61. Dorsey, *Omaha Sociology*, 337.

62. Elder GG, summer 1992.

63. Undated letter from Ed Farley to Francis La Flesche, possibly April 1895. La Flesche Family Papers, NSHS MS2026.

64. Photograph No. RG2039:15, Nebraska State Historical Society, Lincoln, Nebraska. Photograph by Addison E. Sheldon.

65. Hampton University Archives, Hampton, Virginia. Photograph inscribed "Standing Hawk Lodge, Omaha Reservation, Neb. C.W.A.'12." Not available for this publication.

66. Elders RR, MMM, summer 1992.

67. Elder SS, summer 1992.

68. Painter, "Omaha Indian Allotments, 1871," 18; Fletcher," Omaha Indian Allotments, 1882–1883," 181.

69. Mead, *Changing Culture*, 34.

70. The association of supernatural power with the secret societies was an impression that was not limited to only the Omaha. An elder recalled when members of the Marble Society were gathered at the Little Crazy Lodge. There were some spectators in the crowd from the Osage Tribe. One society member was being ritually "shot" but was missed, and an Osage person got hit. The shooter went looking for the stone and retrieved the marble from among the Osage group. The Osages left the lodge in a panic. Elder QQ, as translated by Elder LL, summer 1992.

71. Elder EE, summer 1992.

72. Elder MM, summer 1992.

73. Elder HH, summer 1992.

74. Architectural descriptions of the dance lodge were confined to the most general features by contemporary Omaha elders. Many lodges were remodeled as resources waxed or waned, and were remembered at different stages by the elders.

75. See note 18 above.

76. Elder UUU, autumn 1993.

77. Elder FF, summer 1992.

78. Jerry Maryott Collection photograph on loan to the Nebraska State Historical Society, Lincoln, Nebraska. Jerry Maryott, Decatur, Nebraska.

79. Ralph C. Wilson, *Camera Man and Picture Woman*, Vol. 1, (self published, 1997), 27. Otto Wilson, a Waterloo, Nebraska photographer, created an ethnohistorically rich collection of images of members of the Omaha tribe and Omaha reservation landscape during the 1920s and 1930s.

80. Elder CCC, summer 1992.

81. Elder DD, summer 1992.

82. Elders GG, II, and JJ, summer 1992.

83. Elders II, KKK, summer 1992.

84. Fletcher and La Flesche, *The Omaha Tribe*, plates 59–64, 516–519. Unretouched copies of these photographs were acquired by the Nebraska State Historical Society Photograph Collection from the National Anthropological Archives, Smithsonian Institution. An inspection was made in 1992 by David Murphy, NSHS Senior Research Architect. He noted that the timber posts to which the exterior walls are attached seem to act only as stabilizers against horizontal movement. He suggested the walls could not be bearing the bulk of the roof load.

85. Mead, *Changing Culture*, 28–34.

86. Elders EE, TTT, summer 1992.

87. Fletcher and La Flesche, *The Omaha Tribe*, 324; After 1930: Mead, *Changing Culture*, 29.

88. McEvoy, "Reservation Settlement Patterns," 40.

89. Ibid., 39–41.

90. Prucha, *The Great Father*, 2:759–761.

91. Mead, *Changing Culture*, 62; In the case of the Shell Society, a woman occupied at least one of the critical leadership positions. Fletcher and La Flesche, *The Omaha Tribe*, 516.

92. Elder FF, summer 1992.

93. Elder WWW, summer 1974.

94. Fletcher and La Flesche, *The Omaha Tribe*, 516.

95. A representative collection of the earliest scholarly literature on the Omaha *Hethu'shka* Society and its associated dance can be found in Clark Wissler, editor, *Societies of the Plains Indians*, Anthropological Papers of the American Museum of Natural History, Vol XI, New York: AMNH, 1916. This staggering thousand page volume offers a comparative historical examination of groups throughout the Great Plains with articles by Wissler, Robert Lowie, and Alanson Skinner.

96. Richard E. Jensen, R. Eli Paul, and John E. Carter, *Eyewitness at Wounded Knee* (Lincoln: University of Nebraska Press, 1991), 100.

97. "The War Dance," *Dawes County Journal*, 16 December 1891, 1.

CHAPTER III

Itha paho^n mo^{n}zhi^n
I Had Not Asked About It, 1930–1960

Dance lodges were the arena in which many Omaha customs were practiced. One time-honored Omaha custom is to sacrifice material goods at a public giveaway for the right to dance. An elder recounted the time when his grandmother performed a big giveaway on his behalf at the Wind Lodge, west of Macy. The event took place in the Depression years of the 1930s, in the midst of a social dance. She started her giveaway by ordering the door to be closed. Anyone wishing to leave the lodge before the end of the giveaway had to pledge material goods or food. There was a *wano^{n}she* (soldier) appointed to sit at the door, acting as sergeant-at-arms. Since trying to leave would be expensive, everyone stayed to witness the proceedings. During the giveaway the old woman presented a beef to the Wind organization. The gift was pledged "on the hoof, and ready anytime they wanted to collect it." By sacrificing many material goods in the presence of witnesses, she validated the young boy's right to enter the dance arena. A song was chanted by the singers while the boy and his family danced in the lodge. To conclude the giveaway the old woman ordered the opening of the door. From that day forward, the young boy could take his proper place among the dancers in the arena.[1]

While dance lodges provided a place for social and sacred gatherings, helping to preserve many traditions and customs, they could not protect the Omahas from catastrophic events that confronted the nation in the decades following 1930. Shifting federal Indian policies and the call to arms in World War II impacted the reservation more profoundly than living conditions of the Depression years. Challenges fell upon Omahas in successive waves that forever changed the community. One victim of these years was the dance lodge. Where six structures occupied the Omaha landscape in 1930, only a single lodge survived by 1949 (see Table 2.1).

Which events or crises contributed to this disappearing act? Did the lodges simply fade away, no longer needed by the community, or did their

53

function shift to some other location? What happened to the secret societies and social organizations who filled the lodges with their songs, dances, and prayers? When many elders were asked about tradition and ritual for this era, they responded, "*Itha paho^n mo^{n}zhi^n*, I had not asked about it." This vernacular expression is commonly used to justify a lack of information, or a desire not to verbalize knowledge that might be inaccurate or ridiculed. It is another legacy of the events that buffeted Omaha people after 1930, creating gaps and insecurity in personal knowledge.

The Depression years on the Omaha Reservation were remembered by some as not being significantly different from previous decades. Living on rural allotments, using horses for draft work, tending kitchen gardens, harvesting local native plants, and socializing at neighborhood lodges never required large cash incomes.[2] Whether defined as marginal self-sufficiency or a life of rural poverty, the crash of New York's Wall Street in 1929 did not change the economic expectations of most Omahas.

Outside the reservation, the Depression catapulted Franklin D. Roosevelt into the Presidency on a New Deal platform of economic reforms. Roosevelt appointed John Collier as Commissioner of Indian Affairs in 1933, and they proposed a New Deal for Indians. Collier's New Deal had three objectives: economic development of the reservation and the preservation and increase of the Indian land base, organization of Indian tribes to manage their own affairs, and the establishment of civil and cultural rights for the Indians.[3] Many of the government policies of the early twentieth century that controlled Omahas religiously, economically, socially, and politically were overturned. Collier used executive orders, legislation, and administrative directives as reform tools. Strategies of the New Deal were to reinforce bonds between the Indians and their customs. Banning missionaries from proselytizing in Indian Bureau Schools brought heated debate.[4] Executive orders stressed constitutional liberties in religion, conscience, and cultural matters.[5] These pronouncements were aided by the lifting of many restrictions placed on the reservation. The local Indian Bureau superintendent's exercise of authority in the Courts of Indian Offenses was diminished, making it more difficult to eliminate or suppress cultural practices that were offensive to white officials.[6]

The greatest revolution to Indian policy was the Wheeler-Howard bill enacted into law June 18, 1934. Also known as the Indian Reorganization Act (IRA), it prohibited further land allotments and restored unallotted surplus lands to tribal ownership. The law granted any Indian tribe the right to organize its own government, with appropriate constitutions, bylaws, and corporate charters ratified by a majority vote of adult tribal members. Other provisions addressed education, timber resources, range management, and preferential appointments to the Indian Service.[7]

Each Indian nation was provided the opportunity to vote upon the law prior to it becoming operative. The superimposition of white political structures over existing Indian structures with the goal of protecting Indian culture appealed to younger, more educated whites and Indians who sought the pluralism the IRA proposed. Traditionalists saw the IRA as a threat to their political status. This controversy resulted in 77 tribes (86,365 members) rejecting reorganization. The Omahas were among the 181 tribes (129,750 members) who voted to accept the IRA and set up governments under it.[8] The Omaha constitution and bylaws were ratified by a vote of 311 for, and 27 against, in an election on February 15, 1936.[9] The Omaha corporate charter was ratified on August 22 of the same year by a vote of 221 to 14.[10] Among other points, the IRA instituted an elected tribal council with a broader sweep of economic and political powers.

Elected council members struggled to exercise their new-found powers for the betterment of the Omaha nation.[11] They were faced with a multitude of problems. Tribal population had doubled since the Omahas arrived on the reservation in the 1850s, overcoming periodic epidemics with renewed growth (Table 3.1). A legacy of the allotment process was the passing of lands into heirship. As the original allottees passed away, heirs received title to the land in undivided shares. Disagreements over farming the land and occupying the allotment house increased as more heirs were added to the tract. Leasing the land to non-Omaha farmers proved the most viable alternative. Temporary or permanent abandonment of the home often resulted. Nearly two-thirds of the leased tracts of land in 1955 had more than one heir. Over one-quarter of the tracts had six or more heirs (Figure 3.1).[12] The usable land base continued to diminish, leaving less room for growing families. Councilmen encouraged tribal members to join nearby Civilian Conservation Corps as a short-term solution to crowding and poverty.[13]

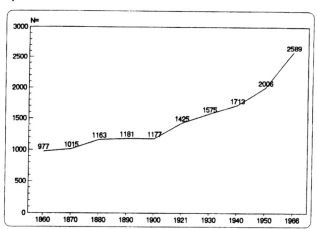

Table 3.1 Omaha Nation Population, 1860–1966. OMAHA NATION POPULATION, 1860–1966.

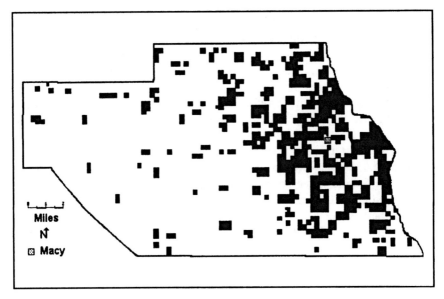

Figure 3.1 Omaha Lands in 1956, Including Tribal and Allotted Parcels. Derived from data in Longwell, "Lands of the Omaha Indians," fig. 17, p. 53.

Insufficient Depression-era aid hindered the tribe's efforts to drive their new government. In 1940, criticism of Collier's New Deal increased. Evidence surfaced among scholarly surveys that reservations were holding Indians in perpetual poverty. The federal government had overestimated the reservation resources.[14] Indian lands could not provide a basis for economic survival for most tribes. Lack of capital and equipment hindered farming or economic development. In 1939 the annual median income for Indian males on U.S. reservations was $500.00, while the annual median income for all U.S. males was $2300.00. (Table 3.2).[15] The need for better incomes lured Omahas off the reservation in search of work. When Work Projects Administration jobs ended at Macy in 1943, many tribal members moved to Omaha. The men drove trucks and taxicabs, worked in warehouses, on railroad section crews, and a few were employed at the Fort Crook plant as laborers. Of the 100 Indians living in Omaha in the early 1940s, the majority came from Macy.[16] Other Omaha families moved to Lincoln, Nebraska, and Sioux City, Iowa, for work in war industries.[17]

Table 3.2 Median Income of Indian, Non-White, and All Males, Selected Years, 1939-1964 (in 1964 dollars)

Year	Indians Non-Reservation	Indians Reservation	Non-Whites	All Males
1939	n.a.	500	925	2,300
1944	n.a.	660	1,600	2,900
1949	1,040	825	1,925	3,475
1959	2,570	1,475	2,950	5,050
1964	n.a.	1,800	3,426	6,283

Source: Sorkin, *American Indians and Federal Aid*, Table I-3, p. 9.

n.a.= not available. Data include all males and all sources of income, whether earned or unearned.

The years bracketing World War II inaugurated as many changes to Native people as did the federal policies of the IRA. When Japan attacked Pearl Harbor in 1941, there were 4000 Indians in military service. By war's end, 25,000 had served.[18] The wartime economy created new jobs off-reservation. By war's end 40,000 persons, one-half of the able-bodied men who had not entered the military and one-fifth of the women, had left Indian lands nation-wide for war related work.[19] Omaha participation kept pace with other tribes. The mass exodus from the reservation into military service and war industries meant that many Omahas earned a decent wage for the first time. One consequence of this out-migration was that returnees were tinged with white cultural values. Nationally, Indian consumerism increased, as did an interest in education, non-Indian religions, and out-marriage.[20] Indian women like their white counterparts were welcomed into defense plant works as riveters, inspectors, and machinists. On- and off-reservation women assumed new roles to replace white professionals and laborers drafted for war. They also replaced their own tribal males who were absent.[21]

World War II was by no means a windfall. It opened the doors for a departure from the reservation of many prominent and dynamic tribal members. Some did not return from the battlefields. Many more followed the lure of wage labor into urban areas. Lack of finances to travel to work sites meant the poorest segment of the tribe stayed home.[22] Shortages of materials occurred on the reservations. Also, many educational and health services were curtailed as professionals were drafted and funds re-allocated toward the war effort.[23]

The Omaha Tribal Council continued to struggle with developing itself under the Indian Reorganization Act. Confusion and conflicts surfaced in 1950 when the outgoing tribal council charged Superintendent H.E. Bruce of the Winnebago Indian Agency with interfering with tribal government. The ability to have a fair council election was questioned.[24] Plagued by dwindling resources, the council launched a land-clearing program east of Macy in an effort to open more arable farm ground from which tribal lease monies could be acquired.[25]

Meanwhile, cultural and ritual functions were undergoing changes. The decline of the dance lodge structure can be attributed to economic, demographic, and political factors. Many cultural and social activities, such as the annual week-long powwow,[26] were suspended during the war. The out-migration of secret and social society members and their lodge-using families removed the financial and physical support necessary for the maintenance of the lodges. Wandering livestock damaged several of the structures, accelerating their collapse. Due to economically hard times and their apparent abandonment, some of the lodges were dismantled for salvage lumber.[27] Dances and other activities were held at smaller venues such as private homes. Some residents in Macy used an old barn located to the northwest of the Tribal Council building as a social hall. A study of the six lodges standing in 1930 shows a period of rapid physical decline. Returning to the ritual east, we can examine each site in clockwise order. All but a single lodge disappeared from the landscape by the late 1940s.

EASTERN QUARTER

SILAS WOOD

Elders recalled the lodge being caved-in and unused in 1936.[28] The earliest aerial photograph in 1938 does not show a lodge on the site.[29] Coupled with the photographs already mentioned, this suggests that the lodge was constructed prior to 1921 and torn down before 1938. After the building was dismantled the survivors of the Shell Society continued to gather at the Wood home to have *xube'wathate*, sacred feasts.[30] These and other social events were held under a canvas arbor.

SOUTHERN QUARTER

WARREN DAVIS/SKUNK/LITTLE SKUNK

Near this lodge a well was drilled to provide water for a five foot circular horse tank. While horses were the most common mode of transportation, cars were driven to this location after 1936.[31] As with most of the other lodges, no land-based photographs have been discovered. A circular building appears clearly in an aerial photograph from 1938 (Figure 3.2).[32] The structure is gone by 1940.[33] Eventually livestock got into the building, and attempts at cleaning their mess failed. The building was reported as abandoned and probably dismantled in the late 1930s.[34] Dances continued to be held on the grounds after all traces of the building had been removed.[35]

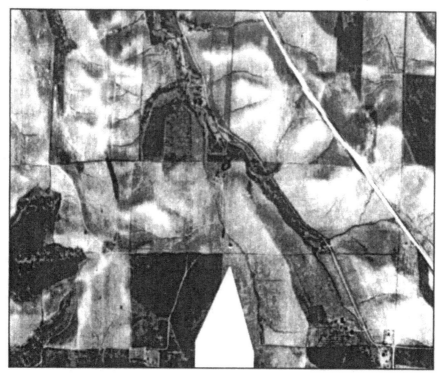

Figure 3.2 Aerial View, Warren Davis Lodge, 1938. (Courtesy Conservation and Survey Division, University of Nebraska-Lincoln, photo no. UW-7-36, Flight 13, 1–5–38, Thurston County).

MATTHEW TYNDALL

Most elders remembered the lodge being used as a horse barn in the 1930s, with many boards missing from the side walls and roof. The surrounding pasture was a popular picnic area for Macy residents. In 1935 the lodge was frequented by children playing on nearby Chase Hill.[36] Aerial photographs from 1938[37] and 1940[38] show a circular structure on the site. The structure is not found in an aerial series produced in the winter of 1944.[39]

WESTERN QUARTER

WIND/BLACKFEET

No land-based photographs have been located for the Wind Lodge. A circular structure is visible on the site in a 1938 aerial photograph (Figure 3.3),[40] validating my Grandmother Elizabeth's recollections and stories which launched the interest in this research project. The horseshoe-shaped clearing is vacant in the 1940 series.[41] An elder suggested that the lodge was stripped for salvage lumber.[42] The rectangular cement stock tank that provided water for the horses was pushed into the creek by a local farmer. A hummock of earth covering the nearby water well was the only visible evidence of the lodge after 1940.[43] Recalling the steam merry-go-round, it has not been determined if the popular dance ground west of the lodge was ever used after the building was dismantled.

Figure 3.3 Aerial View, Wind Lodge, 1938. Note the distinctive "horseshoe" bend in the nearby creek. (Courtesy Conservation and Survey Division, University of Nebraska-Lincoln, photo no. UW-6-293, Flight 12, 1-5-38, Thurston County).

NORTHERN QUARTER

BIG CRAZY/HORSE HEAD

Not all of the lodges disappeared immediately. The newly elected Omaha Tribal Council was called to a public meeting at the Horse Head Lodge in 1942.[44] Local legend tells of a wandering white man who lived in the timber along the Missouri river, using the unoccupied lodge as a place to sleep.[45] The lodge was remodeled and used sporadically into the 1950s, reflecting the shifting resources and interests of the social organizations.[46] Removable wooden shutters were used over the windows in the 1940s.[47] Electric lights were provided in later days. One of the last dances was held in the mid 1950s.[48]

The Horse Head Lodge appears in an aerial photograph produced in the winter of 1944. Under the close examination of a magnifying glass the roof appears in a clearing adorned with patches of snow.[49] An undated and unidentified Otto Wilson photograph (Figure 3.4) is clearly the same structure as a photograph by John Lucius, ca. 1957, that shows the Horse Head lodge in disrepair. Based upon the amount of rolled roofing material that is visible, the Wilson photograph must predate the Lucius image. Both views show that the lodge has been wired for electricity, the cupola is damaged, and the sides of the lodge reveal evidence of unmatched repairs.[50] Weed stubble and encroaching volunteer trees attest to infrequent use.[51]

Figure 3.4 Omaha Dance Lodge, ca. 1933. Joe (Charles) Springer, Mabel Campbell Wilson, and Elizabeth Springer. Photograph by Otto Wilson (Courtesy of Ralph Wilson).

GILBERT MORRIS/LITTLE CRAZY

The lodge stood through the 1930s, but was burned down or dismantled for salvage lumber in the early 1940s.[52] No land-based photographs have been discovered for this lodge. A series of aerial photographs show a circular structure on the site in 1938 (Figure 3.5)[53] and 1940.[54] No structure is visible by a 1944 series.[55] There were no recollections offered of continued dances or activities at the Gilbert Morris home after the lodge was removed.

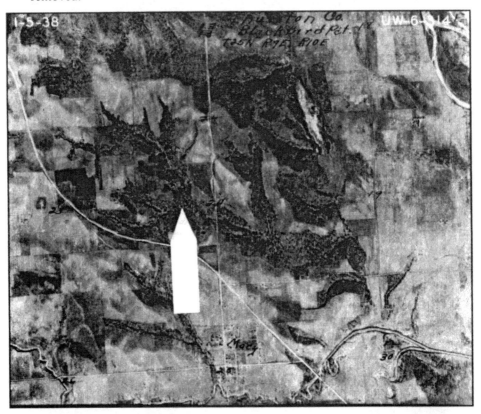

Figure 3.5 Aerial View, Gilbert Morris Lodge, 1938. Note the lodge appears closely surrounded by trees. (Courtesy Conservation and Survey Division, University of Nebraska-Lincoln, photo no. UW-6-314, Flight 13, 1-5-38, Thurston County).

One elder placed the location of the Little Crazies south of Macy in the Decatur area in later years.[56] Another elder recalled that the Little Crazies joined with the Little Skunks, using a lodge north of Decatur at the Warren Davis home. As time passed these organizations discussed the reason for maintaining two separate names. The members decided to combine under the name Little Skunk, and the Little Crazy group ceased to exist.[57]

The merger of social organizations and the disappearance of the lodges can be attributed to the changing population patterns on the reservation (Table 3.3). Between 1940 and 1950, the predominantly Omaha-inhabited eastern reservation township population dropped by one-third, followed by little growth during the next two decades. Rural Anderson township never recovered from the population decline. Blackbird township, including the unincorporated village of Macy and tribal offices, suffered a similar one-third decrease in the 1940s. However, the trend was reversed in the 1970s, with the 1990 population surpassing pre-war figures. The pattern emerges of a rural out-migration coupled with a centralization of Omahas residing in Macy.

Table 3.3 Population by Township, Eastern Portion of Omaha Reservation, 1940-1990

Precinct	1990 Total Pop./ Indian Pop.	1980 Total Pop.	1970 Total Pop.	1960 Total Pop.	1950 Total Pop.	1940 Total Pop.
Blackbird (Macy)	1292 / 1233	1149	953	821	942	1216
Anderson	202 / 129	144	222	213	466	537
Omaha (Walthill)	1212 / 490	1146	1205	1178	1509	1856
Walthill Village			897	844	958	1204
Dawes (Rosalie)	424 / 28	554	616	571	808	873
Rosalie Village			204	182	212	250

Sources: United States, *Eighteenth Decennial Census of the United States, 1960 Census of Population*, Volume 1 Characteristics of the Population, Part A Number of Inhabitants, p. 29-17; *Nineteenth Decennial Census of the United States, 1970 Census of Population*, Volume 1 Characteristics of the Population, Part 29 Nebraska. Issued January 1973, p. 29-30; *1980 Census of Population*, Volume 1 Characteristics of the Population, Chapter B General Population Characteristics, Part 29 Nebraska. PC80-1-B29. Issued July 1982, p. 29-103; *1990 Census of Population*, General Population Characteristics, Nebraska, 1990CP-1-29, Issued June 1992, p. 202.

Many of the families that migrated seventy miles to the city of Omaha were drawn from the southern quarter of the reservation between 1940–1950. They carried an interest in community organization to the urban setting. Two social groups appeared in the city by the early 1950s. The *Xitha'çka*, White Eagle Lodge, was a male group. The English name is attributed to an Indian man from Montana, adopted by the predominantly Omaha members, and a club song composed by Henry Grant incorporated the name rendered in the Omaha language.[58] A leadership dispute resulted in a temporary fission, and a break- away group of younger males organized the Buffalo Lodge. Besides sponsoring handgames and other social events, the Buffalo Lodge assisted newly arrived reservation Omahas with groceries and a week's rent money. The schism was short-lived, and the Buffalo Lodge rejoined the parent group after the departure of a contentious leader.[59]

A female club adopted, or was given, the name *Waho^n'thi^{n}ge*, Orphan Aid Society. Recollections vary about the name's origin. It was transferred to the off-reservation group by Pete Drum[60] or John Miller,[61] with the latter individual composing a song for the club.[62] There is no evidence directly connecting the 1950s urban Orphan Aid Society to the 1920s reservation Orphan Lodge. The women sewed quilts and other items as fund raising measures to support social activities. Their meetings were held separate from the men, but they called upon the White Eagle Lodge to assist in sponsoring handgames. The arrangement was reciprocal, with the women supporting the men's activities.[63]

A general consensus about the urban group name referred to the off-reservation people being "like orphans" due to their residing far from relatives.[64] This characterization may account for the name's undetermined origin with the earlier group. The residents of the southern reservation area near Wood Creek, where the first *Waho^n'thi^{n}ge* group originated, were depicted in 1930 as having their own spatial and social orientation set apart from the people living in or near Macy.[65] This feeling of "distance" or "isolation" is illustrated by childhood stories of a southern resident. Attending a country day school for the first time, an elder recalled the surprise of meeting other children who spoke the Omaha language and hearing of Macy's existence.[66] Northern social groups such as the Big Crazies formalized this sense of distance by referring to visitors from the Wood Creek area as "our southern relatives."[67] Therefore, it can be inferred that the original *Waho^n' thi^{n}ge*, or Orphan Lodge, was named because the organization felt "like orphans" due to their living far from relatives, even when on the reservation.

A pattern of migration between reservation and urban areas emerged as homesickness or other assimilation problems became unbearable.[68] Many urban families came from the Little Skunk area, and both groups maintained complementary socializing arrangements.[69] The formal creation of separate, gender-specific clubs appears as an urban innovation of the Little Skunk practice of gender-specific socialization. It may reflect the growing power of women as they joined other urban workers, their wage earnings serving as a social leveler. The White Eagle Lodge and the Orphan Aid Society interacted and supported each other, suggesting the individuality found in distinctive club names may have been more symbolic than substantive. The important point is that the Skunk Lodge organization is the progenitor of this innovation, even though the Skunk Lodge building had disappeared by 1940. Members and offspring of the reservation group felt confident enough to display their social structure off the reservation by 1952. Both urban clubs remained as separate and complementary groups until the early 1970s, at which time they were restructured as the Omaha Culture Club to accommodate an intertribal membership.[70]

Omahas who moved to the city of Lincoln in the early 1940s were drawn primarily from western and northern reservation neighborhoods. Some of the families that worked in the stockyards during the war years had been participants in the Horse Head, Little Crazy, and Wind Lodges. Several members of the *Hethu'shka zhi^nga* (Little Warriors) dance group joined in this early migration. The 100 mile distance from the reservation made trips to Macy expensive. In response to this isolation the Omaha residents of Lincoln organized a social and self-help group in the early 1950s. Called the Lincoln Indian Club, members gathered in private homes and city parks to play handgame and mark special occasions with family feasting. The name Little Warriors was adopted by a local group of young singers and dancers in the late 1950s. At least one member of the dance group was an original Little Warrior from the reservation.[71]

Many of the policies of the Indian New Deal were reversed after the mid-1940s. In retrospect, the Indian Reorganization Act had not been such a radical shift in policies. Non-Indian constitutions, charters, and organizations continued to assimilate Indians into mainstream society. They did not maintain Indian customs as proposed by Collier.[72] Nor did they really allow Indians to have command of their own affairs. The very election process that the IRA imposed upon the Omahas was still controlled by a non-Indian election board as late as 1959.[73]

With enlistments during the Korean War matching World War II levels, Indian participation in the war effort was seen as a continued move toward mainstream assimilation.[74] Reduced federal budgets meant reservation resources could not support growing post-war populations, nor meet the rising expectations of returning war veterans. Federal policy makers proposed to solve these "Indian" problems with two major programs: termination and relocation.

Termination policies ordered the withdrawal of federal responsibility for Indian affairs, or modified the trust relationship between tribes and the federal government. The Wisconsin Menominee led the list of tribes selected for termination in 1954.[75] Omahas became alarmed in 1958 when the Bureau of Indian Affairs discussed transferring many Omaha services to county and state agencies, as well as moving the Omaha Indian Agency away from the reservation. Tribal Council Chairman Alfred Gilpin summed up the people's fears in a newspaper interview when he suggested that Congress would not pass legislation to terminate the Omaha Tribe. Instead, the same effect would be achieved by the Bureau of Indian Affairs taking away agency services and selling Omaha lands.[76] While the Omahas escaped termination, they were fully aware of the results such policies had upon their neighbors - lands were lost, federal management and property protection were withdrawn, state and local authority were imposed, and any special Indian health, education, and welfare programs were discontinued. The loss of identity as Indians was a severe psychological blow, and the specter of termination would act as a catalyst in the following decades for tribal sovereignty movements.[77] Feelings of helplessness and panic resurfaced when the Northern Ponca, neighbors and kin of the Omahas, were terminated as a tribe in 1962.[78]

The relocation program was promoted in the 1950s in an effort to reduce crowding on reservations, and increase the assimilation process. As a continuation of the termination of federal responsibility in Indian affairs, the program encouraged permanent movement to urban areas such as Denver, Chicago, Dallas, and the west coast. Job training and housing assistance did not address the many problems that arose from the relocation process. While some Omahas took advantage of the program, most preferred to seek work in nearby urban areas where relatives already lived.[79] By 1956, 121 Omaha families resided in the city of Omaha. The poorer parts of the city were better than the sub-standard housing without running water available on the reservation.[80] The existence of Omaha-oriented social groups, such as the Lincoln Indian Club, White Eagle Lodge, and Orphan Aid Society, helped to bridge the gap between cultures.

Thirty years of tribal government reorganization, world war, termination, and relocation brought great changes to the Omaha people. As more allotment lands entered heirship status, the rural population moved closer to Macy or off-reservation. Every three years a newly elected tribal council was faced with providing services to a coalescing community with dwindling resources. In 1958 the Omahas were harshly characterized by an urban journalist as being "among the most culturally disintegrated and socially ill in the country. In their bleak community at Macy, Neb., the eight hundred residents were a divided people, barely able to recall the last time they all did something together."[81]

This pessimistic, inaccurate, and overblown pronouncement, seems typical of an outsider's superficial view. It could be answered with an insider's assessment of the situation. Tribal Council Chairman Alfred Gilpin pointed out that the Bureau of Indian Affairs had taken care of the people in a way that made them forget to take care of themselves. He said, "Today (the Omahas) are just waking up and beginning to hate this helplessness."[82] Community changes could be seen in the decline of nineteenth century secret and social societies as members aged or departed for the Armed Forces and off-reservation jobs. They were replaced by numerous new social organizations. Some of the new groups were recognized as branches from existing lodges. The *Çka A'gthi[n]*, White Riders, were associated with the Horse Head Lodge in the north.[83] The *I'xasto[n]*, or Opossums, were a southern group with connections to the Skunk Lodge.[84] The smaller groups gathered at private homes for handgames and moccasin games, while occasionally providing players for shinny ball games.[85] They were the result of fissioning or members pursuing their own socializing interests. A group which surfaced for a short period included the *Mo^{n}çe çka wano^{n}p'i^n*, Money Necklace, or Silver Necklace people who took their names from the distinctive medallions they wore.[86] An ephemeral men's social group in the southern reservation area was known as "The Quiet Bunch,"[87] while a group of young girls in Walthill, Nebraska, were known as the "Short Skirts."[88]

New organizations such as the World War II Minute Women (begun ca. 1942) followed by the War Mothers revealed the contemporary consciousness of the tribe interpreted and expressed through traditional roles. Omaha consciousness, or cultural self-awareness, has surfaced since 1960 in several forms, since the Omahas entered an era of self-determination and cultural revivalism. A stronger tribal council provided new initiatives, organization, and services to the Macy community. From the tribal council level down to the individual tribal member, many are attempting to bridge the gap in traditional knowledge from previous generations—lost to social upheavals reaching back to the earliest reservation days. These modern efforts have been watched with mixed emotions by the elders. It is in this setting that the final chapter will look at the tradition of the dance lodges on the modern Omaha landscape. With the absence of all but one building by 1960, how do the memories of the lodges and their secret societies shape today's Omahas? What did these turn-of-the-century structures leave as a legacy for future generations? Where do the dance lodges fit in a period that has been characterized by some elders, tongue in cheek, as the time when "*itedi nikashi^{n}ga ukethi^n go^{n}tha*," now they want to be Indians?

NOTES

1. Elder DDD, summer 1990.

2. Elders RRR, WWW, summer 1974; Elders AA, YY, and NNN, summer 1992.

3. Alison R. Bernstein, *American Indians and World War II: A New Era in Indian Affairs* (Norman: University of Oklahoma Press, 1991), 5–6.

4. Prucha, *The Great Father*, 2:951.

5. Bernstein, *American Indians and World War II*, 9.

6. Prucha, *The Great Father*, 2:951–954.

7. Ibid., 2:962–963.

8. Bernstein, *American Indians and World War II*, 7–8.

9. United States, Department of the Interior, Office of Indian Affairs, *Constitution and Bylaws of the Omaha Tribe of Nebraska*, Approved March 30, 1936 (Washington: Government Printing Office, 1936).

10. United States, Department of the Interior, Office of Indian Affairs, *Corporate Charter of the Omaha Tribe of Nebraska*, Ratified August 22, 1936 (Washington: Government Printing Office, 1936).

11. Elders LL, MM, winter 1993.

12. A. R. Longwell, "A Thesis: Lands of the Omaha Indians," (M.A. Thesis, Department of Geography, University of Nebraska-Lincoln, 1961), 54–61.

13. Elder TTT, winter 1993.

14. Bernstein, *American Indians and World War II*, 10.

15. Ibid., 15; United States, Bureau of Indian Affairs, "Reservation Income, 1939," (1939, unpublished), 2 as cited in Alan Sorkin, *American Indians and Federal Aid* (Washington, DC: Brookings Institute, 1971), 9.

16. J. Harold Cowan, "Jobs Attract Indians to City," Omaha, NE *World-Herald*, 17 October 1943, A7.

17. Elder TTT, summer 1992.

18. Bernstein, *American Indians and World War II*, 40.

19. Ibid., 67–68; *Annual Report of the Commissioner of Indian Affairs, For the Year 1944* (Washington: Government Printing Office, 1944), 237.

20. Ibid., 60–63.

21. Ibid., 73.

22. Ibid., 75.

23. Ibid., 81.

24. "Omaha Indians Name New Council," *World-Herald*, 5 November 1950, 12, Omaha, Nebraska.

25. Elder LL, summer 1992.

26. The annual powwow is held in August. Tribal members set up camps under the shade trees for a period of handgame playing, dancing, singing, feasting, and socializing. Elders recall earlier powwows lasting from seven to ten days. This may reflect an era when people came early to set up camp and remained after the formal program was concluded. The contemporary length is four days, Thursday through Sunday, in deference to people working during the weekdays. Favorite campsites are retained by families through traditional usage, and trespassers are soundly harangued. Individuals and families will host feasts and giveaways to mark special events or achievements of the previous year. The tribe or certain individuals will provide meals for visitors through the course of the powwow. Sessions of dancing are held each afternoon and evening. Contemporary powwows place a growing emphasis on contest dancing, while diminishing time spent on giveaways and feasting.

Elder WW, summer 1992, recalled that people used to camp in the powwow grounds in their lodge groupings. Big Crazies and Little Crazies together on the north side of the grounds. Blackfeet were to the west. Wind Lodge and the Money Necklace groups were along the southern fence, near the entrance gate. Author's note: the location of the northern and western groups appear to have a connection to where the physical lodge structures were, relative to the location of the powwow grounds.

27. Elder II, summer 1992.

28. Elder FF, summer 1992.

29. Conservation and Survey Division, University of Nebraska-Lincoln, Lincoln, NE, Photograph No. UW-6-312, Flight 13, 1-5-38, Thurston County. Hereinafter cited as CSD Photograph.

30. Elder MMM, summer 1992.

31. Elder FF, summer 1992.

32. CSD Photograph No. UW-7-361, Flight 14, 1-5-38, Thurston County.

33. CSD Photograph No. UW-1A-45, Flight 8, 9-2-40 Thurston County.

34. Elder FF, summer 1992.

35. Elder KKK, summer 1992, reported dancing at the Warren Davis place about 50 years ago, aged early 20s, and there was no lodge. Author's note: This is consistent with the 1940 aerial photographs which confirm there was no lodge by that time.

36. Elder JJJ, summer 1992, remarked "The steep hill that the road cuts through coming south out of Macy was named for Hiram Chase. It was a popular sledding hill in the winter, being possible to coast the nearly one-half mile to the Blackbird Creek bridge and beyond. The lodge was used as a place to warm-up in the winter. Some of us built fires inside the lodge. Our mothers would have disapproved."

37. CSD Photograph No. UW-6-312, Flight 13, 1-5-38, Thurston County.

38. CSD Photograph No. UW-1A-125, Flight 6, 9-2-40, Thurston County.

39. Aero Service Corp. Collection, Nebraska State Historical Society, RG4979, Photograph No. 1400-142-8, October 1944-May 1945. The Aero Service Corp. of Philadelphia, Pennsylvania, produced a series of glass plate negative images of the Missouri River corridor extending from Bellevue, Nebraska in the south to Yankton, South Dakota in the north. The collection includes series of images from low, mid, and high altitude.

40. CSD Photograph No. UW-6-293, Flight 12, 1-5-38, Thurston County.

41. CSD Photograph No. UW-1A-123, Flight 6, 9-2-40, Thurston County.

42. Elder CCC, summer 1992.

43. Author's personal observations, 1971–1974.

44. Elder LL, summer 1992.

45. Elder LL, summer 1992.

46. Elder GG, summer 1992. "Parties interested in repairing and using the Horse Head Lodge would come and ask permission. They were always encouraged to use the lodge, as that was the purpose of the structure."

47. Elder LL, summer 1992.

48. Elder MMM, summer 1992.

49. Aero Service Corp. Collection, Nebraska State Historical Society, RG4979, Photograph No. 1400-145-7, October 1944–May 1945.

50. Photograph in author's possession. Photograph by Pastor John Lucius, Phoenix, Arizona. Reverend Lucius was stationed in Macy, 1954–1957.

51. Elder TT, summer 1992.

52. Elders EE, TTT, summer 1992.

53. CSD Photograph No. UW-6-314, Flight 13, 1-5-38, Thurston County.

54. CSD Photograph No. UW-1A-123, Flight 6, 9-2-40, Thurston County.

55. Aero Service Corp. Collection, Nebraska State Historical Society, RG4979, Photograph No. 1400-139-8, October 1944–May 1945.

56. Elder TTT, summer 1992.

57. Elder II, summer 1992. Author's note: The use of the lodge at the Warren Davis home after the dismantling of the lodge at the Gilbert Morris home seems problematic. The Warren Davis lodge was absent in the 1940 aerial photographs, while the Gilbert Morris lodge was still standing at that time.

58. Elders TTT, XXX, and YYY, spring 1994.

59. Elder TTT, spring 1994.

60. Elder FF, summer 1992.

61. Elder ZZ, spring 1994.

62. Elder XXX, spring 1994.

63. Elder TTT, spring 1994.

64. Elders FF, summer 1992; Elder ZZ, spring 1994.

65. Mead, *Changing Culture*, 34.

66. Elder YY, summer 1992.

67. Elder MMM, summer 1992.

68. Bernstein, *American Indians and World War II*, 79.

69. Elders YY, ZZ, summer 1992; Elder TTT, spring 1994.

70. Elders TTT, XXX, spring 1994.

71. Elders NNN, OOO, summer 1992.

72. Bernstein, *American Indians and World War II*, 19.

73. "Tribe Picks 14 in Primary," *World-Herald*, 17 September 1959, 9.

74. Donald L. Fixico, *Termination and Relocation: Federal Indian Policy, 1945–1960* (Albuquerque: University of New Mexico Press, 1986), 57.

75. Prucha, *The Great Father*, 2:1046–1048.

76. "'Chief' Fears End of Tribe," *World-Herald*, 27 April 1958, B11.

77. Prucha, *The Great Father*, 2: 1049.

78. Ibid., 2:1046–1048.

79. Elder TTT, spring 1994.

80. Robert Agee, "Many Omahas Now Omahans: Indians Leave Reservation, But Their Problems Pile Up," *World-Herald*, 1 July 1956, G16.

81. Joy Miller, "Omahas Take Control of Tribe Rehabilitation," Ibid., 2 September 1958, 2.

82. "'Chief' Fears End of Tribe," Ibid., 27 April 1958, B11.

83. Elders GG, II, JJ, YY, and ZZ, summer 1992.

84. Elders GG, LL, summer 1992.

85. Elder YY, summer 1992.

86. Two related stories described the *Mo^{n}çe çka wano^{n}p'i^n*, Money Necklace, or Silver Necklace people who took their names from the distinctive medallions they wore. Elder WW, summer 1992, recounted how two Tribal Council members or appointed delegates went to Washington, D.C. They received silver dollars and made them into necklaces. When these men returned with the medals, it was claimed they received the medals for selling the tribe [lands]. Both men were thrown out of the lodge windows, suggesting the practice of holding tribal meetings in the lodges.

Elder ZZ, summer 1992, recounted that the people warned them (delegates) not to let Uncle Sam (the United States Government) put the necklace on them, but they came back with the necklace on, and the Omahas lost their land.

Elder YY, summer 1992. The necklace was also described as a big "nickel," with a man's face on it.

Elder WW, summer 1992, placed a Silver Necklace (Lodge?) in the draw, on the road to Blackbird Hill, southwest of Macy.

87. Elder YY, summer 1992. "*Wai'azhi*, the 'Quiet' group was just like other [neighborhood] groups. All of the members came from surrounding families. Some members came down from Macy and included themselves in the group."

88. Elder ZZ, summer 1992. "We little girls used to play handgame. We used to play in Macy, too. We stayed there [in Walthill] just over the winter. We'd all play handgames in Grandma's middle room. Uncle took care of the sticks. Mom said Slim Parker sang for us. Soon it got to be a regular group. We'd bring cookies, and Grandma would make coffee. We'd spend our evenings that way. Older women joined in. An older lady called 'Emma Ute' used to like to get dressed up. She wore her squaw dresses real short, and used make-up. They gave us the name *Wate'xe*, or *Wache'xe*, Short Skirts. It got bigger and bigger, and us little ones got shut out. I don't know if they continued after we left [Walthill]."

CHAPTER IV

Itedi nikashi^{n}ga ukethi^n go^{n}tha:
Now They Want to be Indians, Since 1960

On a hot June day in 1961, 500 people jammed the tree-shaded powwow grounds at Macy to join Nebraska Governor Frank Morrison at a tribal celebration. The Governor's visit was part of his state-wide promotion of tourism. The Omahas enthusiastically supported his efforts, and the June festivities launched a summer-long series of Indian dances and ceremonials. Scheduled for every Saturday and Sunday afternoon, they were designed to entertain visitors while aiding the tribe's economy. At this well-publicized event, the Governor received a ceremonial pipe from the Chairman of the Tribe, and was invited to return to receive an "Indian" name during the August annual powwow.[1]

Where the tribe had been characterized two years before as ". . . culturally disintegrated and socially ill . . . a divided people,"[2] now they were presenting a positive profile for non-Indians in the region. Part of this change can be attributed to major shifts in federal policy. Federal termination policies of the previous decade were slowly scrapped in favor of programs for economic development and self-sufficiency. Nationally, emphasis was placed on industrial development and building recreational facilities that would attract business to the reservations.[3] The Omahas took the opportunities that were offered from these new policies, combined them with their own creative energies, and produced tribal programs and initiatives that were uniquely Omaha. A proposal for a massive tourist development project, including motel, museum, art center, visitor's bureau, and trading post, was indicative of the direction the Omahas were willing to pursue.[4]

The new era of Indian self-determination was a catalyst for a stronger, centralized tribal government, able to wield greater influence over the affairs of individual tribal members. One example of this influence could be seen in where dances and rituals took place. The Omaha Tribal Council emerged as the provider of services or space for many of the secular and sacred activities of the community. These efforts were given a boost from the outcome of a ruling from the Indian Claims Commission. The Omahas had presented a case in the 1950s against the United States Government charging inadequate compensation for the over 7 million acres of Iowa and Nebraska lands ceded under the treaties of 1830 and 1854.[5] In 1962 a $2.9 million settlement was received by the Omaha Nation for the lands taken. After a $750 per capita disbursement was made to the enrolled members, the balance could be applied to tribal programs and projects that had long suffered from a chronic shortage of funds.[6] One of the first projects to be funded the following year was a community building/gymnasium, complete with a kitchen.[7]

While the community building was under construction, the tribe launched a second project that would create space for the tourist-oriented ceremonies and dancing that had continued at the powwow grounds since 1961. Dubbed the "Omaha Mission Recreation Area," the new site was located along the Missouri River two miles northeast of Macy. Roads were bulldozed to provide access to camping sites and a marina. Bleachers built of stout bridge planking would surround an amphitheater for the Sunday afternoon dances. Hiking trails were planned to provide access to the old Presbyterian mission site, cemetery, and fresh-water spring that gave the development project its name.[8]

The new recreation area was less than one-quarter of a mile east of the Horse Head Lodge. However, a visitor driving along the country roads on the Omaha reservation would have had a difficult time locating the building. The two-wheel ruts that skirted Horse Head Creek leading to the lodge were choked by chest-high grasses and over-hanging branches. The grassy clearing around the structure had been replaced with a bottle-littered thicket of stinging nettles, raspberry bushes, and climbing wild grape vines. The underbrush, together with the encroaching canopy of trees, successfully concealed the building on its rise of ground. The shake shingled roof sagged under the combined weight of age and winter snows. Except for an infrequent visit by curious children on school outings,[9] the Horse Head Lodge faded further into the past. Abandoned a few years before as unrepairable, the Horse Head Lodge social group held activities in a rectangular shed at the nearby Walker home, or convened at Macy.[10]

The community building was completed in 1964, but progress on the recreation area was hampered by the lack of all-weather roads.[11] The Omahas overcame the problem by combining their project with a federal development plan to create 70 public recreation access areas along the Missouri River extending from Sioux City, Iowa, to St. Louis, Missouri. Renamed "Chief Big Elk Recreation Area," Governor Morrison applauded the Omahas for becoming one of the first groups to co-sponsor a portion of the regional tourist development project. At the 1966 ground-breaking ceremony, the Governor sweetened the victory by approving the establishment of a Neighborhood Youth Corp which would employ 55

Omahas to develop the recreation area and a nearby tribal farm.[12]

Besides providing employment opportunities and space for community activities, successive tribal councils tackled other problems on the reservation. Programs to develop adequate housing, health, and sanitation began with three modest family homes in 1962.[13] Two years later, construction began on a $300,000 water and sewage system in Macy.[14] By 1966, the Omahas dedicated the completion of a 30-unit housing project named "Sun Rise Village,"[15] and a health clinic soon after.[16]

Land losses due to the allotment process could not be easily reversed. On the other hand, some Omahas saw a clear case of land loss that could be corrected. The center of the Missouri River channel had been designated as the reservation's eastern boundary under the terms of the 1854 treaty. When the seasonal movements of the river were stopped by flood control projects after the turn-of-the-century, several thousand acres of Nebraska farm land were left stranded on the Iowa side of the river. Being too difficult to access by the impoverished Omahas, the lands were taken over by non-Indian farmers in Iowa. Energized by their successes of the 1960s, the Omahas started to press a claim for the return of 4,480 acres of Iowa land,[17] a process that would take fourteen years of endeavor.[18]

Proceeds from land claim cases allowed the tribe to fund many self-help projects of the 1960s[19]. However, decisions about how the funds were disbursed and who was eligible to use the health, education, housing, and loan programs they supported, fueled debates among tribal members. At stake was the fundamental question of what constituted a member of the Omaha Tribe. Members having less than one-quarter Omaha blood had been dropped from the rolls, and did not receive shares of the original land claim money.[20] The disbursement of land claim awards in subsequent years was questioned for the same reason.[21] Lively interest on such topics resulted in a major overturn of the tribal council in 1962 elections,[22] and again in 1965.[23] These controversies only helped to demonstrate the magnitude and complexity of the problems faced by Omaha people as they grappled with self-determination strategies.

Involved with issues such as these, it is no wonder that the final disintegration of the Horse Head Lodge drew little notice. Heavy snow storms in 1969 overburdened the aged structure, reportedly bringing the roof down to the ground in a single stroke. A photograph the following summer showed the single center pole standing guard amidst a welter of shake shingles and split rafters.[24] This process of decay would continue unabated so that by the summer of 1992 only vestiges of a circular wooden roof surrounding remnants of a brick chimney could be found at the site.[25]

With the collapse of the Horse Head Lodge, an era of neighborhood-based buildings on the Omaha Reservation seems to have come to an end. Structures and space used for social and secular activities have since been provided by the tribal government body, including the community building, powwow grounds, and Native American Church hall. As the ruins of the last dance lodge melt back into the earth near Horse Head Creek, what is the legacy, if any, of these unique structures that once dotted the Omaha landscape? Where do they fit in today's Omaha culture?

The strongest personal image of dance lodges rests in their intangible association with sacred people and sacred acts. The elders of today treasure memories of the secret societies and social groups of earlier days. Especially strong are the memories of the activities in which their own parents participated, and in which they were witnesses as young children. As they observe undesirable changes in their contemporary surroundings, the dance lodge days offer a nostalgic picture of an "idealized" traditional Omaha lifestyle. Images of proud relatives, dressed in nice clothes, are typical and sincere.[26]

A related intangible legacy of the lodges are unarticulated feelings of awe and wonder at the power of the "old people." Coupled with the mysterious abilities of the secret society members is the belief that the ancestors followed a disciplined, moral code that has somehow slackened in modern times.[27] Such feelings and images are strongest among the elders, becoming diminished and underdeveloped among the majority of the younger generations. However, the association of the dance lodge with a more "traditional" value system can be found in the stories told by some of the younger community leaders.[28]

On a more tangible level, the lodges served to protect and nurture ritual space through years of external assault. Blending into the architectural environment of the dominating non-Indian culture, lodges did not draw threatening notice from neighboring whites (Figure 4.1).[29] They provided the ritual space in which dances and ceremonies could be conducted at a time when such practices were coercively suppressed. This maintenance of key cultural practices contributed to the pool of contemporary memories from which today's culture is drawn.

The lodges illustrated Omaha adaptive abilities. Residential patterns from the allotment process tended to isolate people on individual parcels of land. One response to this imposition was the florescence of pre-existing groups including the Shell and Pebble Societies. Other neighborhood-oriented organizations such as the Little Skunks, Orphans, Blackfeet, Big Crazies, Little Crazies, and Little Warriors were created. They came to replace the diminished tribal institutions, the Sacred Pipes, Sacred Pole, and Tribal Packs, as maintainers of tribal cohesion and unity.

Using an innovative approach, some of these groups and individuals constructed buildings that blended earth lodge designs with modern techniques and elements. Carpentry skills taught by the Indian agent as an avenue toward assimilation were turned to the task of fashioning traditional ritual space. Materials, land, and labor were all donated by private

Figure 4.1 Omaha Dance Lodge, undated. Inscribed "Dance House," Omaha Reservation, O-21. (Courtesy of Hampton University Archives,).

sacrifice in a manner that was distinctively Omaha. Ownership of the lodge was modified to each situation, resting with individuals as well as groups (Figure 4.2).

While serving to resist cultural change, the lodges provided an arena for selective acculturation. Euro-American holiday activities, Christmas trees, Halloween masquerades, and birthday celebrations were some of the outside concepts accepted into Omaha culture. Reconfigured to fit the Omaha world view and translated into the native language, these ideas were sanctified and normalized by their admission into the dance lodge.

The societies and lodge structures could not turn back the transformations of world war and relocation policies. Out-migration, rural neighborhood depopulation, and shifting economic conditions diminished the viability of the dance lodges. However, they had served their purpose well. They had protected and promoted dances and ceremonies in an uninterrupted line from past generations. Their robust, pro-active treatment of ritual space was transmitted to the newly organized tribal council. The construction of the community building and maintenance of the powwow grounds continues the cycle of dance and ceremony in Omaha culture.

Figure 4.2 "The Four Children," Members of the Shell Society, before 1910. Note the seated individuals in the background. The lodge roof and sidewalls are constructed of milled lumber. The wall is supported by a native timber post. From Fletcher and La Flesche, *The Omaha Tribe*, pl. 59, facing 516 (Courtesy National Anthropological Archives, Smithsonian Institution).

By the close of the twentieth century the continuing evolution of a stronger centralized tribal government is linked with an increasing number of individuals willing to publicly express their vision of Omaha culture. Feelings of increased group sovereignty and individual self-esteem have supported the tribal government's efforts in repatriating Omaha human remains held in several public collections. As well, this rebirth movement has been the catalyst for the restoration of ritual materials back to the community. Perhaps the most publicized of these has been the return of two items of cultural patrimony from American museums, the Sacred Pole in 1989, and the Sacred White Buffalo Hide in 1991.[30]

Many aspects of Omaha culture and ritual are being reformulated and expressed in the public sector. While the public education system remains an institution of national hegemony and national ideology, the Macy Public School has been recently renamed as the Omaha Nation Public School as a symbolic gesture of cultural reclamation.[31] This symbolism is further enhanced by most community members, students, and faculty using the Omaha language to pronounce the name as "*Umo^nho^n* Nation."

Inside the school Omaha cultural practices and values are being more vigorously inserted into the standard curriculum.[32] An Omaha Culture Center has been established within the school to help locate community resource people willing to assist the students and teachers. Community elders act as role models in the classroom while disseminating cultural knowledge. Although the use of Omaha language remains low, sporadic, and problematic, other culturally loaded symbols are more widely used. These include reifying the Omaha clan system with its associated list of personal names, community responsibilities, and taboos. Pre-reservation subsistence practices, especially bison hunting, are being used to organize class themes and areas of study. The *Hu'thuga*, or ceremonial camp circle from the communal buffalo hunt days, has reappeared on T-shirts and posters as a visual model of student body unity.

Other activities in the greater Omaha community show evidence of the cultural renaissance. The *Xthexe'*, or Mark of Honor tattoo, and its associated *Hoⁿ'hewachi* Society had a long relationship with certain dance lodges. With those lodges gone, only a few elderly women alive today with the Mark of Honor, and no process for new membership, it would be easy to imagine the society quickly fading away. However, the role of the "blue spot" women in Omaha society as "...people who were supposed to be good to the poor and the sick", especially orphans, remains a strongly held value.[33] In 1993, the tribe built an emergency youth shelter to help troubled families and youths. Named The Mark of Honor Youth Lodge, its staff carries forward the tradition of care for the less fortunate children of the community through its direct reference to this ancient society.[34]

The August powwow remains a central period of social and ritual activity for the Omaha tribe. It depends upon dance lodge era and other antecedent practices for its strength.[35] Its purpose and significance continues to evolve in order to fulfill contemporary ideas about Omaha tradition and identity. While it continues to be identified with the *Hethu'shka* Society dance, in recent years the four day autumn gathering has begun to be referred to as the *He'dewachi* (Festival of Joy).[36] In pre-reservation days the *He'dewachi* Ceremony was held in the summer "when the plum and cherry trees were full of fruit" and "all creatures were awake and out."[37] This re-assertion of the powwow as an ancient ceremony is related to the renewed interest in Omaha history and culture, especially as it has been interpreted through historic and ethnographic texts.

The importance of ritual and ritual space has survived. From the early earth lodges and hide tepees, through the wooden dance lodges, to the brick and cement community buildings, the Omahas continue to adapt their available resources to meet cultural needs. Their manipulation of space follows the circular practice of bygone earth lodge days, despite the mixture of straight-sided building patterns. It will never truly matter what shape or material is used in a building. The Omahas will always enter from the east and proceed clockwise around their ritual circle of life.

＊ ＊ ＊ ＊ ＊ ＊ ＊ ＊ ＊ ＊

On June 6, 1993, members of the $I^{n}ke'çabe$ (Black-Shouldered Buffalo Clan) assembled at Macy, Nebraska.[38] The gathering occurred because the sponsor felt a need to identify the clan relatives, to learn about the clan's historic and modern-day role in the Omaha Nation, and to share a family meal. While this first-time ever gathering was an innovative approach to cultural inquiry, it was conducted in a traditional manner similar to meetings and feasts held at dance lodges long ago. The sponsor discussed the propriety of such a novel gathering with several clan elders. After receiving approval and encouragement to pursue the idea, a weekend date was selected to accommodate clan members traveling from urban areas. Despite rainy weather and other scheduled activities, approximately 50 persons came to the Alfred W. Gilpin Community Building for the meeting and meal.

The sponsor and two male relatives arrived early in the morning to prepare the building for the event. The area was cleared of litter and the floor swept and mopped. Expecting a small number of participants, the long rectangular gymnasium floor was shortened by placing a row of benches across the center, creating a more intimate square area on one end. As clan members arrived, many carrying their own folding chairs and dishes, they seated themselves around the smaller area. More people entered the room, maneuvering the benches and chairs to create a circular form.

Meat and dried sweet corn for soup, coffee, and cookies were provided by the sponsor. The task of cooking was performed by female relatives at a nearby home, using large metal boilers placed over an open fire. Firewood for the event was donated, along with other side dishes and the all-important frybread. The food was delivered to the community building and placed in the center of the seated group. At that moment the circle became a traditional ritual space, and children were directed to play quietly behind the benches or outdoors.

A blessing for the food was offered in the Omaha language by the eldest Buffalo Clan male. After the invocation, the food was served to the circle by younger clan members. Out of respect for the servants, no one began to eat until all had received their portions. Latecomers were served as soon as they found a place to sit. Conversation was reserved while everyone attended to eating. When all had been served, leftover food was distributed to the most needy families present. As an added gift, the sponsor's cooking utensils and serving dishes were given away to elderly females. Accumulated litter and empty serving dishes were moved out of the center of the circle, and the area cleaned. At this point group discussion began.

The sponsor stood and addressed the gathering, acknowledging elders in the room, donations of food, help from the cooks, and every other individual in attendance. The four broad reasons for the gathering were recounted. After apologizing for any mistakes in organizing or conducting the meeting, the sponsor sat down. After a period of polite silence and introspection, elders began to stand and speak in turn. Each gave thanks to the sponsor for calling the gathering, and relatives and other elders were greeted in the circle. Some of the speakers related stories that illustrated a portion of the clan's traditional history or tribal responsibility. Others provided narratives concerning their own personal clan name. Still others spoke of the clan's duty toward contemporary issues facing the Omaha Nation. All provided powerful oratory, while the gathered circle paid respectful attention. Except for some light-hearted teasing by the elders, no one was interrupted or ridiculed. This lively exchange lasted for an hour. The discussion ended with Buffalo Clan members considering plans for another gathering in the near future.

After the building was vacated, and the overhead lights extinguished, all that remained of the day's events was a circle of benches on the darkened gymnasium floor. A non-Omaha encountering this arrangement might be at a loss to decipher the significance of this form. Like a turn-of-the-century photograph of a circular building, a dance lodge on the Omaha landscape, it would seem enigmatic or inconsequential. But, to a traditional Omaha person entering the cement and brick building, the circle of benches would speak eloquently of living ceremony. Out of respect for all of the ancestors and their traditional ways, an Omaha person would walk a clockwise path around that circle of ritual life.

NOTES

1. Tom Allan, "Indian Visit is High Spot: Governor's Touring Group to Macy," Omaha, NE *World-Herald*, 11 June 1961, B14.

2. Joy Miller, "Omahas Take Control of Tribe Rehabilitation," Ibid., 2 September 1958, 2.

3. Prucha, *The Great Father*, 2:1091.

4. "Tourist Post to Aid Indian," *World-Herald*, 3 November 1961, 29.

5. Walter Rowley, "The Omahas Sue U.S.," Ibid., 4 May 1958, G4-G5. Note: The award was announced on February 11, 1960; 6 Ind. Cl. Comm. 730 (1958), Docket 225A. Omaha Tribe and Nation v United States.

6. "3,000 Share Tribe Award: $750 Each To Go To Omaha Indians," Ibid., 14 January 1962, B6. Note: this article inaccurately reports that the Indian Claims Commission award was for lands taken in the 1880s. The judgement was for lands taken under the Treaty of 1854. See note 5 above.

7. "Tribe Starts Gymnasium: Ground Breaking at Macy Program," Ibid., 4 August 1963, B6. For an in-depth examination of this Indian Claims Commission case and aftermath see: Scherer 1999:47–67. The community building, was renamed the Alfred W. Gilpin Community Building in the 1990s. A late 1960s era photograph of the structure appears in Steven Standingwater, *People of the Smokey Waters: the Omahas* (Macy, Nebraska: n.p., 1970:12). Photograph by John Michael Mangan.
8. Tom Allan, "Land of Omahas, Winnebagos, A Visitor Bonus," Ibid., 12 January 1964, B12.

9. Elder BBB, summer 1992.

10. Elders KK, LL, summer 1992.

11. "Indians' Progress Pleases 'Big White Father'," *World-Herald*, 6 June 1964, 6.

12. Tom Allan, "Omahas Hold Powwow, Break Ground at Macy," Ibid., 25 May 1966, 10.

13. Tom Allan, "Indians at Macy Build and Plan," Ibid., 29 September 1962, 4.

14. "Indians' Progress Pleases 'Big White Father'," Ibid., 6 June 1964, 6.

15. Tom Allan, "Indian Lodge Now Modern," Ibid., 12 February 1966, 23.

16. "Macy Clinic Dedicated," Ibid., 3 May 1968, n.p.

17. "Omaha Indians Want Two States to Know Land Is Theirs," Ibid., 11 February 1966, 23.

18. Fred Thomas, "Indian Land Rule Has Wide Impact," Ibid., 15 January 1980, 1; For a description of the Blackbird Bend case see Scherer, *Imperfect Victories*, 89–114.

19. Conservation and Survey Division, University of Nebraska-Lincoln, Lincoln, NE, Photograph No. UW-1-MN-181, Flight 4, 6-26-71, Thurston County. This photograph clearly shows new community developments such as Sunrise Village, Skunk Hollow and Tower Road housing areas, a waste water settling pond east of Macy, and newly-graded cemetery roads.

20. "Indians Schedule Walthill Meeting," *World-Herald*, 9 August 1962, 19.

21. "Tribe Award is Questioned," Ibid., 27 July 1965, 8.

22. Tom Allan, "Old Council Is Voted Out: Only Two Re-elected by Omaha Tribe," Ibid., 6 November 1962, 6.

23. Tom Allan, "Tribal Council Is Elected," Ibid., 3 November 1965, 47.

24. Standingwater, 1970:9. Photograph by John Michael Mangan.

25. In 1992, nearly 8 feet of the lower brickwork remained upright, the balance being scattered in chunks on the south side of the site. While the upright chimney had been skewed over the years, it appeared to have its four corners oriented to the cardinal points. The red chimney bricks bore the manufacturer's mark "CLA-ROC." These bricks were reportedly manufactured after 1910 by the Sioux City Brick and Tile Company, suggesting the addition of the chimney anytime after that date. See: Karl Gurcke, *Bricks and Brickmaking* (Moscow: University of Idaho Press, 1987), 216–217.

The roof was composed of simple rafters and cross pieces to which cedar shake shingles were nailed. There was a row of overlapping galvanized ridge caps at the joints of each roof panel. There was no evidence of horizontal joists or trusses between the side wall and central pillar. A single peeled log pole, 12 inches in diameter and 18 feet long, rested on the ground. With its butt end near the chimney, it stretched towards the north. Approximately 8 feet from its base were nailed several metal cable clamps, similar to the type used on telephone poles.

There were two remnants of a sidewall at a distance of 22 – 24 feet from the chimney. A 4 foot high stump from a natural timber post was set into the ground on the east side of the lodge. A vertical row of rusting nails were exposed along the side. Another short stump on the north side included a fragment of milled wood nailed vertically to its side. The growth of volunteer trees of any size remained outside of this sidewall perimeter. Midway between the second stump and the chimney rested a rusty metal barrel stove.

26. Elder SS, summer 1992. "Everyone dressed 'nice' in the old days. Women wore broadcloth dresses. They had braids and beaded dangles that joined together to make three pendants. These were finished with dime pendants. They had black shawls with Italian brocade that were sold in local stores. The men had simple outfits, one or two feathers in their headdress, like straight dancers. Everyone acted 'nice,' with no running around in the arena."

27. Elder XX, summer 1992. The lodge users in the old days followed a strict code of behavior. Two elders recounted stories about tardiness. One description of this code tells about a man being late to deliver a hog he had donated for a Little Skunk activity. He was "punished" for his tardiness by having to crawl around the interior of the lodge on his hands and knees.

Elder TTT, spring 1994. Another point of conscientious behavior included each group member providing his or her own utensils for eating. A sergeant-at-arms would inspect everyone's dishes. Each person was to have a cup, bowl, plate, spoon, salt cellar, and napkin. Persons lacking an item would be singled out for good-natured punishment. Since married couples would often try and place the blame for any dish oversight on their spouse, both would be penalized. One form of chastisement included having the wife take her place in a man's seat at the drum. She would be expected to sing a song. Her husband would dance in the arena, usually with many whimsical movements.

Elder TTT, spring 1994. Smoking inside of lodges was regulated. Persons wishing to indulge would pay ten cents for their first cigarette, and a nickel thereafter. A cup would be provided for people to ante-up each time, and the proceeds were given to the sponsors of the activity or the group treasury.

28. Informant ZB, fall 2000. A younger minister of the Native American Church illustrated the changing Omaha attitudes of proper behavior in the event of a death on the reservation with the following story: In this particular case, a man came to a dance lodge where a hand game was already being played. Rather than coming inside, this individual peered into the windows and doorway, obviously looking for someone who was inside. The man-in-charge of the event noticed the activity at the door and directed the sergeant-at-arms of the sponsoring organization to inquire what the man wanted. The sergeant-at-arms went outside and spoke to the man, who relayed the message that "so-and-so's relative had just died." The sergeant-at-arms informed the man-in-charge of the development. The hand game was immediately stopped and the drum put away. All of the food which had been gathered

for the event was distributed to the people in attendance. Rather than eating the food in the dance lodge, everyone collected the food into bundles and the crowd quietly dispersed to their homes.

Today, there is an increasing practice of holding dances, feasts, and other social events while a body lies in state for the four days prior to the funeral. As the story was meant to show, in earlier days all activities would cease while the body was above ground. The explanation traditionally given was that the drum should be silent, and sounds of gaiety subdued, out of respect for the bereaved family.

29. An unidentified Omaha Dance Lodge, undated. Inscribed "Dance House," Omaha Reservation, O-21. Courtesy of Hampton University Archives. Note the whole log construction of the walls. Another unidentified dance lodge is featured on the cover of Lee, Dorothy Sara and Maria La Vigna, editors, *Omaha Indian Music: Historical Recordings from the Fletcher/La Flesche Collection.* The booklet accompanies the Library of Congress American Folklife Centers 1985 re-recording of Omaha music from wax cylinders to long- play vinyl discs and cassette tapes. The image is titled "an Omaha gathering near Macy, Nebraska, ca. 1890 (Courtesy of the Presbyterian Historical Society). The image features an unidentified lodge at one end of an oval of tepees and tents set in a shallow valley flanked by hay meadows and corn fields. A cleared grassy area on the opposite end of the oval appears to serve as a dance arena. As of early 2000, neither the Presbyterian Historical Society nor the American Folklife Center have been able to confirm the origin of, or current disposition of, the original image.

30. Ridington and Hastings, *Blessing for a Long Time,* 70, 200; A 30 minute video documentary focuses on the Pole's return, including some of the feelings of ambiguity expressed by the Omaha community. *Return of the Sacred Pole,* Native American Public Broadcasting Consortium.

31. Cordes, Henry and Lisa Prue, "Reservation School Faces Long Climb Out of Neglect," *Omaha World Herald,* 15 Feb 2000, 1, 6.

32. Examples of culturally relevant curriculum materials include: Elmer Blackbird, et al *Omaha Youth Math and Science Activities* (Lincoln: Nebraska Math & Science Initiative, 1994); Patty Amgwert *The Omaha People: The Teachers Guide for an Encounter Kit for the Omaha Tribe* (Lincoln: University of Nebraska State Museum 1990[?]); and a series of at least nine booklets written by students and translated into Omaha by the Culture Program elders, produced by the Macy Public School, 1987–1989, and funded under the Title IV, Indian Education Act.

33. Omaha elder Pauline Tyndall, as quoted in Ridington and Hastings, *Blessing for a Long Time,* 168.

34. "Mark of Honor Issued First 2 Year License," *Signals,* July/September 1995, 10.

35. See Chapter 3, note 26 above.

36. *Dancing to Give Thanks* (Lincoln: Nebraska ETV Network, 1988); "190th Umo[n]Ho[n] Nation Harvest Celebration" (Souvenir Program), Macy: Omaha Tribe of Nebraska, 1994, 11; "191ST UMONHON HE'DEWACHI" *Signals,* April/June 1995, 12.

37. Fletcher and La Flesche, *The Omaha Tribe,* 251.

38. The gathering of the *I[n]ke'çabe* (Black-shouldered Buffalo) Clan was sponsored by the author.

Afterword

Fifteen years have passed since the memories of more than fifty Omaha elders were gathered and woven together to tell this story about the dance lodges. Today, only one in three of those elders remain with us. All of the elders whose interview transcripts are preserved in these pages have left us for the next world. While there is sadness at each passing and the associated loss of cultural knowledge, it is the natural course of life that we must accept. We who remain behind must carry on the traditions and teachings that have been gifted to us by our elders.

The University of Nebraska Press's request to reprint the story of the Omaha dance lodges provides an opportunity to update the Omaha case and to look at other research on the topic since 1992. Since this book focuses almost exclusively on the Omaha dance lodges, I solicited information about lodges in other parts of the Great Plains. I circulated an e-mail message to the SiouanList, a group of scholars and students of the vast Siouan language family, asking if anyone was familiar with lodges in their region. A number of people responded with visual images, firsthand knowledge, and anecdotal information. I am grateful for their input.

Clyde Ellis of Elon University described dance lodges among various Oklahoma tribes, including the Poncas, Osages, Otoes, and Kaws. Agency records of the early twentieth century were indicated as useful sources of information on the construction of lodges. He noted in 2007 that the Poncas had just built a new round house in White Eagle, Oklahoma.

Tom Leonard in Tulsa forwarded images of Ponca and Osage dance lodges and Osage peyote round houses extant in the early twentieth century. He mentioned the possibility of a lodge among the Quapaws. If such is the case, dance lodges can be attributed to the five Dhegiha relatives: the Omahas, Poncas, Osages, Kaws, and Quapaws. Leonard reported that quite a few people still remembered the details of lodges that may no longer exist. He also forwarded several on-line sources, such as the Library of Congress website, that contain images of dance lodges.

Billy Maxwell, Randy Graczyke, and Jimm Goodtracks contributed notes about dance lodges among the Hidatsas, Otoes, Pawnees, and Crows. John Carter at the Nebraska State Historical Society reminded me of images of dance lodges among the Sioux people in the John A. Anderson Collection. Three images from that source are included here. He also forwarded another reference to an "Omaha Dancing House" at Wounded Knee, South Dakota, in the first decade of the twentieth century.[1] This may coincide with the army map of the Wounded Knee battle site noted on page 44. In the upper right-hand corner of the map is a six-sided structure with the caption, "The Omaha."

A crucial piece of information came with the discovery of Peter Nabokov's "Hidden Blueprints" article. In this paper he describes the appearance of circular dance lodges throughout the Great Plains, Great Lakes, and California since the late nineteenth century. It may well be the seminal work on this topic. It is a fantastic comparative piece that anyone interested in cultural diffusion and cultural resistance should read. The endnotes are as interesting as the body of the narrative.

Nabokov does not mention any Omaha dance lodges directly. However, the Omahas figure prominently in his description of the spread of the Hethushka (Warrior) Society Dance. Transmitted and transformed as it moved from tribe to tribe, it became known by many names, including the Grass Dance, Hot Dance, and Omaha Dance. Male societies were created to perpetuate the performance of the dance with its distinctive regalia. Each tribe added elements of other rituals to make the dance their own. Prestige offices were established that permitted some members to carry a quirt or sword, blow bone whistles, wear the hair roach, and display the unique "crow belt" or bustle. However, the multitude of stories and interpretations surrounding the origins of the Hethushka/Grass Dance deserve their own telling and are beyond the scope of this paper. Consult Nabokov's endnotes for citations of many of the major works on the Hethushka/Grass Dance.

What is important in the Nabokov analysis is the relationship between the spreading Hethushka/Grass Dance and the concomitant spread of the wooden dance lodge. From the early 1880s until the Indian New Deal of the 1930s, Native peoples experienced extreme pressure to assimilate into mainstream white society. The outcome of the land allotment process was different for each tribe, as illustrated by the following two examples.

In the Omaha case, taking allotments scattered the people across the landscape. It is suggested in this book that the increased distance to a central ceremonial location may have encouraged the emergence of neighborhood groups who built lodges for rituals and entertainment. Tom Leonard suggested that allotment for the Poncas in Oklahoma did not create a complete dispersal of people. He reported that many Poncas chose to camp communally at the Ball Diamond by the present-day powwow grounds, where they remained into the 1960s. Tribal government reorganization in the 1930s impacted the role of hereditary leaders. Localities may have replaced or contended with the role of the clans.[2]

We find the emergence and spread of the Hethushka/Grass Dance throughout the Great Plains during this period of darkness. It is clearly an example of Native perseverance and ingenuity. Tribes continued to visit tribes. Ideas, dances, regalia, and societies were exchanged. The Ghost Dance of this era engendered fear among whites, as evidenced by the federal response at Wounded Knee Creek, South Dakota. On the other hand, the Grass Dance is characterized by Nabokov as less overtly ideological and "might be credited as one of Native America's most ingenious survival strategies." He concludes that "Grass Dancing endured because outsiders were often ignorant that it was going on. . . . Some of the male-only Grass Dance groups found it advantageous to pound those drums away from prying eyes—behind closed doors and wooden walls."[3]

He recalls how Clark Wissler described "a dancing house of definite form" as a key trait of the Pan-Indian Grass Dance complex.[4] Anecdotal stories from Omaha elders tell of the Hethushka Dance being held regularly in most of the local dance lodges. The elders surmised that when visiting tribes saw the dance and wished to acquire it, they took with them the idea of the building that it was housed in. In the Omaha case we have an image of an early unidentified lodge built of logs (figure 4.1) similar to some of the earliest log cabins built by Omaha people after moving to the reservation in 1855–56. In 1871 the Omaha people experienced their first allot-

Captioned "Woman preparing rawhide from which parfleche was made." Note in the background the log cabin house typical of the Sioux reservations for this period. (Courtesy John A. Anderson Collection, Nebraska State Historical Society, photo no. RG2969.PH:2-226)

Captioned "Woman preparing a meal." Unidentified location on the Sioux Reservation. Note the log round house in the background. (Courtesy John A. Anderson Collection, Nebraska State Historical Society, photo no. RG2969.PH:2-203)

ment under provisions in the Treaty of 1854. By the time they underwent the second allotment in 1882, many Omahas were building milled-lumber homes and barns. The transition in housing materials and architectural treatments is mirrored in the construction of dance lodges dating since that period.

Construction materials for lodges among the Sioux appear to correlate with materials used in home construction. In his final endnote Nabokov marvels at the number of images of lodges that magically appear after one becomes sensitized to their existence. This is the case with images from the John A. Anderson Collection at the Nebraska State Historical Society. A preliminary survey of this large collection focused on the foreground actions or persons identified by the photographer's captions or notes. Only upon closer scrutiny does one notice the unobtrusive log dance lodges in the background.

Nabokov closes his paper with the observation that the dance lodge remains an understudied architectural phenomenon. He notes that "their construction process and ceremonial uses in different tribal culture-histories remain under documented and often beyond research. . . . Probably hundreds of these structures went up and came down without a trace."[5] I wish to add my voice to the call for further research into the dance lodge phenomenon within and between all of the tribes of the Great Plains and

Captioned "Omaha Dance or Grass Dance June 2, 1889, Fort Niobrara, NE," also marked "Rosebud Agency, S.D." A penciled note questions attribution of John Anderson as the photographer as he never filmed in Chadron. Note the distinctive Hethushka-style dance bustles. (Courtesy John A. Anderson Collection, Nebraska State Historical Society, photo no. RG2969.PH:2-116)

American West. It is hoped that this story of Omaha dance lodges contributes to that larger body of knowledge.

Nabokov's conclusions are similar to those suggested in this Omaha case study. The Omaha lodges appear to have served as camouflage and bastions of cultural maintenance in a time of intense social, political, and spiritual strain. As tribal institutions were eclipsed by federal policies and practices, the lodges arose to provide ritual space. In their daily walk of life, Omaha people wore "citizen clothes," spoke English, lived in milled-lumber homes, worshiped at various Christian churches, and sent their children to school to learn English and the American lifestyle. Within the lodges Omaha people could be themselves, honor their heroes, sing their songs, and speak their language. The lodges declined in the 1940s through a combination of factors, including the out-migration of energetic families seeking economic opportunities in nearby urban areas, the World War II experience, and the growth of a stronger centralized tribal government.

When the Omaha research was finished in 1994, it was distributed to all of the contributing Omaha elders—twenty-five years after the collapse of the last remaining Omaha dance lodge, the long-abandoned Horse Head Lodge north of Macy. Since then, brief references to the dance lodges have emerged occasionally during public oratory at dances, feasts, and the annual August powwow. A few younger adults have engaged me in conversations about the lodges. The general direction of these discussions was about how someone would construct a lodge today. Related questions arose about who would own, finance, and control it. To date, there is no evidence that indicates any plans for building a lodge are being seriously considered.

Ritual space continues to be provided and maintained by the Omaha tribal government. The Alfred W. Gilpin Building, constructed in the 1960s, is the primary interior space. The Powwow Arena, nearby Small Arena, and the surrounding campground are the open-air venues for warm-weather gatherings. The local chapter of the Native American Church has acquired the old Veterans of Foreign Wars building for prayer meetings and memorial feasts. The gymnasium of the newly expanded Umonhon Nation Public School has been pressed into service for funerals requiring more space than the Gilpin Building can provide.

Unlike the late nineteenth and early twentieth centuries, there is no group-, society-, or family-owned gathering place today. It may be that, unlike other tribes of the Great Plains, the Omahas no longer see the need for separate dance lodges dedicated to the Hethushka Dance and other social activities. The Omaha Hethushka Society underwent a brief revival in the late 1970s and early 1980s. It waned during the 1990s. Recent efforts to increase membership and determine the modern role of the society are preliminary but hopeful. However, with ritual space already being provided by the tribal government, it is unlikely that the Hethushka Society will attempt to muster the determination and resources to build a lodge of their own. For the Omahas, dance lodges may truly be places of memory.

Notes

1. Richard E. Jensen, ed., *The Settler and Soldier Interviews of Eli. S. Ricker, 1903–1919* (Lincoln: University of Nebraska Press, 2005).

2. Tom Leonard, personal communication with author, May 8, 2007.

3. Peter Nabokov, "Hidden Blueprints," *North Dakota Quarterly* 64 (2000): 265.

4. Clark Wissler, "General Discussion of Shamanistic and Dancing Societies," *Anthropological Papers of the Museum of Natural History* 11 (1916): 862, quoted in Peter Nabokov, "Hidden Blueprints," *North Dakota Quarterly* 64 (2000): 265.

5. Peter Nabokov, "Hidden Blueprints," *North Dakota Quarterly* 64 (2000): 304.

Appendix A
Roster of Sacred and Social Group Members

The following list of individuals attributed to various social or sacred groups was compiled from interviews with Omaha elders. The names may represent informal usages. Some individuals were referred to only by a term of relationship, out of respect for the Omaha custom of not speaking the name of a deceased relative. It should be considered as a working list, presented here to stimulate further memories. Additions and corrections are encouraged. The author apologizes for any spelling errors.

Mo^{n}ga (or) *Mo^{n}ga i^{n}sh'age* (Old Skunk):
Stewart Walker
Sam Gilpin
Benjamin Walker - Tenugazhi^{n}ga

Mo^{n}ga zhi^{n}ga (Little Skunk):
Nebraska Hallowell
Ernest Smith
Henry Lovejoy
Sam Harlan
Tom Walker
Stewart Walker
Alec Walker
Henry Walker
Tecumseh Dick
Henry Guitar
Charlie Guitar
Paul Freemont

Bertram Freemont
John Lyon
Charlie Grant
Fred Baxter
Frank Baxter
Mitchell Dick
George Dick
Smoke Morris
Henry Lasley's father, a Pottawatomie
Sam Gilpin
George Mitchell
Dave Mitchell
Roy Mitchell
Clyde Hallowell
George Blackbird
Robert Smith
Alec Esau
Cabney? Pappan
Walter Peabody
Charlie Edwards
Henry Grant and Lizzie Brown
Carrie and Pete Drum
Martha Drum
Phillip Porter
Jonas Walker

Waho^n'thi^{n}ge (Orphan):
Ed Blackbird's father and mother (Pete? and ?)
Bertram Freemont
Paul Freemont
Dave Canby
Neal Mitchell

Waho^n'thi^{n}ge (Orphan), remembered as a *Xube wachigaxe* (Sacred Dance):
Bertram Freemont
Frank Leaming
Bert Baxter
"Old Man" Smoke (Morris?)
No^{n}gtheze
Horace Kemp and wife

I'xasto^n (Opposums):
Herbert Duvall
Ed Miller
Charlie Parker
Francis Parker
Logan Parker
Jim Freemont
Sam Kemp
Horace Kemp
Ed Cline
Frank Leaming
Pollock Parker
Silas Hallowell
Thomas McCauley
John Kemp

Wai'azhi (Quiet):
Joseph A. Gilpin
Sam Gilpin
Morgan Grant and son
Charlie Grant and sons

Tade' (Wind):
Parrish Saunsoci and his wife Clementine
"Big" John Lyon
"jim" Nicholas Lyon
Theodore Morris
Suzy Morris White
Charles Robinson?
The Black Family
Ella Robinson and John Wolfe
John and Albert Robinson family

Çiçabe (Black Feet):
Theodore White, Sr.
Jim McCauley.
Valentine Parker, Sr.
Harrison Harlan, or Henry Harlan, the father.
Frank Cayou
George Robinson
John Robinson

Sam Robinson
John Wolfe
Harry Solomon
Alfred Blackbird?
Tom Reese?
Sam Black?
Charlie Grant

Washish'ka athi^n (Shell Society):
Tom Mitchell
Maggie Johnson's uncle
Bertram Freemont
Horace Kemp

Gtho^{n}thi^n ton^{n}ga (Big Crazy):
Mr. and Mrs. Sarpy Saunsoci
Mr. and Mrs. Norman Saunsoci
Charlie Walker
Elizabeth Lyon
Mr. and Mrs. Lute Smith (Winnebago)
John and Suzette Turner
Henry Turner and Jennie Woodhull
Theodore Morris, Sr.
Hazel Morris (Northern Ponca)
Mary Lieb Mitchell
Abbie and Freddie Merrick
Theresa Nolan
Alfred Blackbird?
Elton Mitchell
Ben and Louie Saunsoci's father
Charlie Springer
Bert Mitchell
Ted Morris
Sam Parker
Ben Parker
Henry Parker
Paul Lovejoy
Joe Parker
Issac Springer
Issac Sherman
Joe Walker
Charlie Walker

Bill Walker
Bill Lovejoy
Jacob Parker
Charlie Parker
Henry Parker
Sam Parker

Gtho^{n}thi^n zhi^{n}ga (**Little Crazy**):
Gilbert Morris
Sam Parker
Theodore Morris, Sr.
Henry Turner
Theodore White, Sr.
Dan Walker
John McCauley
Ben Parker

Çka a'gthi^n (**White Riders**):
Henry and Anna Parker
Ralph Dixon
White Webster
"Old Lady" Kemp, *Teo^{n}wi^n*
Henry F. Grant
Lizzie Brown Freemont Grant

Minute Women:
Lizzie Lieb Springer
Mary Lieb Mitchell
Susan Lovejoy Robinson
the 4 Wood sisters
Blanche Harvey
Lucy F. Grant
Eva McCauley
Mary Grant
Florence Merrick
Susan Dick Robinson
Caroline Miller Lovejoy
Bertha Webster Miller
Norman Ann Dick's Mother (— Mitchell Parker)

War Mothers:
Lizzie Lieb Springer
Alice Cayou
Mary Clay
Lillian Dixon Wolf
Suzette La Flesche Turner
Edith Warner

Mo^{n}çe çka wano^{n}p'i^n (Money Necklace):
Paul Freemont
Bertram Freemont
Charlie Guitar
Andy? or Annie? Guitar
Issac Sherman
George Mitchell

Wate'xe (or) *Wache'xe* (Short Skirts):
Irene Harlan Gilpin
Rachel Sheridan
Ida Parker
Mr. and Mrs Clyde Sheridan, Sr.
Mr. and Mrs. Ed Cline
Lillian and Clyde Sheridan, Jr.?
Fay Morris
Mary Grant
Mamie Grant
Mr. and Mrs. Albert Preston
Margaret Woodhull
Ruth Grant
Jack Thomas
Slim Parker
Addie and Dorothy Warner

Hethushka zhi^nga (Little Warriors):
Henry Saunsoci
John Turner
Louis Webster - drumkeeper
George Parker
Morris Hastings
Elton Mitchell
Charles Stabler, Jr. - custodian
Logan Walker
Filmore Walker
Forrest Fields
Sam Harlan
Harry Solomon - advisor
Paul Thomas
Dave Blackbird
Adam Grant
Sam Cook
Theodore Morris, Sr.
Charles Parker
Tom Reese
Theodore White, Sr.
Gilbert Morris
Carey La Flesche
Levi Levering
Henry Turner
Guy Stabler, leader of the last buffalo hunt
Clyde Sheridan, Sr.
Sam Parker
Henry Parker
Ben Parker
Pollock Parker
Albert Robinson

Appendix B
Oral Interview Transcripts

Of the nearly 50 Omaha elders who contributed to this story in 1992, several granted permission for their interviews to be placed on audio tape to facilitate my note-taking. In each case, the elder requested copies of the tapes for their family's use. In every case, the elder granted permission to have their name associated with the dance lodge project. These interviews provide an invaluable insight into Omaha culture and history. To be able to hear the voices, inflections, banter, and laughter makes the rendering of these stories both touching and delightful. In the Spring of 2001, there is only a single surviving elder who shared dance lodge stories on tape. Thus it makes the act of listening to these recordings even more bittersweet.

In order to reproduce these taped interviews, and out of respect for the memory of each of the deceased elders, every effort has been made to secure a re-affirmation of permission from an appropriate member of each family. To these families I give my thanks.

The individual recollections are shared here with the intention of providing clear and articulate Omaha voices to an otherwise composite reconstruction of a cultural phenomenon. I would assert that oral histories are as much about remembering "facts" and "dates" as they are about providing a personal connection to, and explanation of, the past. Future scholars are encouraged to note the sometimes diverse explanations for historic events or cultural concepts reflected in these narratives.

The narratives are presented in the order in which they were recorded because the nature of my interview questions reflect information gained from previous interviews. The aim of this approach was to verify information already received. This is a dynamic process, but can be biasing. Most of the false starts, redundancies, socially sensitive references, or clearly unrelated materials have been deleted for ease of reading. English translations for the Omaha material have been included wherever possible. Otherwise, the speaker's communication style has been left unaltered.

I wish to acknowledge and thank the series editors, John Wunder and Cynthia Willis-Esqueda, for recommending and supporting the inclusion of this material as appendices to the Dance Lodge story. Financial support for the transcription of these interviews was provided by the University of Nebraska Institute for Ethnic Studies, the Native American Studies Program, and the author's family.

TOM C. WALKER
June 18, 1992

Thomas Carson Walker was born and raised in the rural area south of Macy, Nebraska in 1907. My early relationship with Tom C. has already been described in the opening acknowledgment section of this paper. Tom C. was asked to participate in the dance lodge project due to his publicly recognized interest in Omaha history, his senior and respected stature in the Macy Senior Citizens organization, his articulate speaking abilities in both English and Omaha, and his own personal interest in pursuing the topic when the project was first announced to the elders. Tom C. accompanied me on many interviews, acting as both counselor and interpreter. He was interviewed in his home at Macy, Nebraska.

An introductory history...

MR. WALKER: Well, when you hear about the way back then, in the early days, when the Omaha tribe lived in different clans, they lived in a circle, sort of a powwow like. They lived, oh, probably — they might of lived on a hill or on a level elevation. But the Ho^nga, they were the first clan. They were the first ones. And the rest, they all followed each group. And they camped by themselves. And that one time, they had this snow storm that come along, and blowed. Naturally, the Ho^nga got the snow drift. So, they were drifted in. And that's what they call Ho^nga *umubthi* [When the snow drifts into the tents of the Ho^nga; January]. And through that, it's been known that way through that clan, Ho^nga. Ho^nga *umubthi*. Meaning, that they were drifted in. So, from that, why they figured that they were the head ones. And the rest of the clans followed.

But still, the tribe had a leader. One time, some way, some how they had another leader, and according to what they say, them two leaders got into a disagreement and this second leader took off and — and some of the Omaha tribe followed him. And the original tribe stayed because we're the ones that stayed here on this reservation. On this central part of Nebraska.

But then they say that way out north somewhere, there's a tribe there, I think, I don't believe they called themselves the Omahas, but they talked the same. We'd go over there and we'd talk to them and they understand. We understand each other. But their tribe is a different name. Of course, now, the other tribe that took off, there wasn't very many of them. But the original tribe, they stayed here on the reservation.

Of course, they went way down south and all around and wherever they camped, well that was the place where they claimed. One of them that I heard them say was, "Bellevue, Nebraska." And they come on up this way and I forget, now, just where it is — But anyway, them towns wherever they stopped and camped for a while, they came further north and that place and that town, that came, originally it built up and they called it *Maobthe*, was one town that they called *Maobthe*.

And the name that I heard, but then I just don't remember right at the present time, but still there's some — the towns around the reservation like Walthill, Nebraska, they called it *To^nwo^ngtho^n tega*, new town. It just started up. And how come that town got its name is a farmer lived there on that 40 acres. And his name was Walter Hill. His house was there for a while, but now it's gone. They probably tore it down or what, I don't know. But then that's the town that's on the reservation now, Walthill, Nebraska.

And then, going further north, is a Homer, Nebraska. There the Omaha camped there and made a camp site there. And while they were there, quite a few of them, even to the young kids, took sick and died. And they have a burial some where, I think — I don't know in what direction, from the present town, but still, they had a cemetery there where they buried their deceased ones. But just a while back, they dug up some of them old graves and they dug up the bones and gathered them up and they had them down to Omaha. And that's where, when they went down there, they had one of our prominent leaders here on the reservation, and that was Clifford Wolfe, Sr., came down there, asked him in their own belief, to burn cedar and smoke them bones and bury them again. So, that's some of the old traditional activities that I heard. Where they went to Omaha to burn seeds for them bones, I was there. But still, that's the way it is, I guess.

And another time, I went with my son. My son was on the council — Omaha Tribal Council. He had to go down to Omaha for some meeting. And after the meeting, they mentioned Logan Fontanelle. And they asked if they had any descendants. And naturally, I spoke up and I introduced my son as one of the tribal men — tribal councilmen. Then, there was a woman there, she had said she had vests that Logan Fontanelle had on when he was killed. So, I seen the vest. I wished that I had put that vest on for size, but I didn't. That's another experience that I had. Through that, I was proud, at least, that I was proud of my great grandpa, Logan Fontanelle.

And, of course, on the reservation, Logan Fontanelle had two daughters. One was Mary and the other was Sue. Susan is my grandmother. And Mary is these Lovejoys on the Omaha tribe. She had kids and now her grandkids and great-grandkids are here on the reservation.

That's some of the things that I know and that's about as much as I can say. So, I hope that things will turn out better for our tribe, now. Before we had project jobs, working on the reservation and had some water dams built on the reservation and things like that. And they gave us road work and we were just living good. But some way something happened that they cut off that program and now everybody is jobless. No job, no work. And it's been that way for the last few years now. So, I wish things would turn out better so at least my family and my kids, my grandkids, great-grand-kids would have a better life. But as for myself, I'm old now, and I can't get around and jump around like I used to. I'm way up in 85 years. Of course, I hope to live longer. I hope to hit 100. Amen.

Dance lodges...

MR. WALKER: This lodge — This first lodge is up north, here. But it's so old it caved in, now. I think that's the Wind Lodge, I believe. Either that — or Big Crazy.

MR. AWAKUNI-SWETLAND: [consulting a topographic map] Here's the Gilbert Morris place. Do you remember that lodge there?

MR. WALKER: The lodge was a little ways from the side.

MR. AWAKUNI-SWETLAND: And then you continue on north [on the gravel road north of Macy]. If you turn back east, Ramona Turner's place is here. [But continuing north] come back here, here's the turn-in road. Right there is a lodge. Do you remember that one?

MR. WALKER: Yeah. Yeah. I've been there a few times. I was one on the council in '42, I think, I was on the tribal council. They had a meeting there and we were just newly elected. And it's like we are here, talking, and we had to tell who we were and what our intentions were about tribal matters and one thing and another like that. That's where we had a meeting and I remember that. It was at that lodge.

MR. AWAKUNI-SWETLAND: At the Horse Head Lodge, 1942, more or less?

MR. WALKER: Yeah.

MR. AWAKUNI-SWETLAND: Can you describe what the inside of that lodge looked like?

MR. WALKER: Well, I don't think it was finished inside.

MR. AWAKUNI-SWETLAND: So, you could see the outside — you could see the walls and —

MR. WALKER: And two-by-fours.

MR. AWAKUNI-SWETLAND: And two-by-fours?

MR. WALKER: Yeah.

MR. AWAKUNI-SWETLAND: Just a ring of two-by-fours with wallboard.

MR. WALKER: Yeah, and then a little outlet, you know. Where if they should have to eat or something, where they cook back in there.

MR. AWAKUNI-SWETLAND: Oh, there was? Kind of a kitchen?

MR. WALKER: Kind of a little place there where they cooked.

MR. AWAKUNI-SWETLAND: Do you remember what side of the lodge that was on? The door was on the east, right?

MR. WALKER: Yeah, the door was on the east side.

MR. AWAKUNI-SWETLAND: Were there windows that you recall?

MR. WALKER: Yeah, there were windows — the square windows, just so far apart all the way around.

MR. AWAKUNI-SWETLAND: So, if you walked in on — if you were walking in the door from the east, that cooking area would be where?

MR. WALKER: It would be at the east.

MR. AWAKUNI-SWETLAND: If you walked in on the east side?

MR. WALKER: Yeah, it would be like this here would be the lodge [showing me the arrangement by moving objects on the table in front of us].

MR. AWAKUNI-SWETLAND: Right.

MR. WALKER: This here would be that little like kitchen-like and past that — and after that is the lodge.

MR. AWAKUNI-SWETLAND: Okay, so it was right near the front door, just on the south side?

MR. WALKER: This door right here. That's the only entrance. In them early days, you know, lodges, they had their regulations. And some way — I forget just how it is, but if one guy disagreed on something, he'd cut that door off. Otherwise, he shut that door. He shut that door with a horse.

That would have been in the early days. But that's the law, an Indian law. And some of those guys, they either got to, in order that they wanted to get out, they'd have to get up and give that man something. And then again, if there's another guy there, in the crowd, if he's well equipped or he's got livestock, maybe he'll get up and say, "I open that door with a beef."

MR. AWAKUNI-SWETLAND: Okay.

MR. WALKER: See, that's a law there, too. And all those who have got to be excused [need to use the outdoor bathroom], boy, they sure go for the door.

MR. AWAKUNI-SWETLAND: So, you and me, we're in there with a whole bunch of people and for some reason you want something to happen, you could close the door to make everybody stay in there?

MR. WALKER: Yeah.

MR. AWAKUNI-SWETLAND: You close the door by putting your horse up there, or something. And so sooner or later, whatever it is that needs to be done is going to get done before somebody is going to open that door again?

MR. WALKER: No, before.

MR. AWAKUNI-SWETLAND: Before.

MR. WALKER: Just like I say, a lot of them's got to be excused, but they can't get out. So, somebody comes up and saves the crowd and he opened that door with a beef, or something like that.

MR. AWAKUNI-SWETLAND: What happens to the thing that's given, the beef, the horse, who gets that? Where does it go?

MR. WALKER: Well, the guy that closed the door, that's what he wanted. He wanted the people to give him something. But before that happens, well that guy over there will open the door.

MR. AWAKUNI-SWETLAND: When you walked into the Horse Head Lodge at that time, in 1942, what kind of floor did it have?

MR. WALKER: Ground floor.

MR. AWAKUNI-SWETLAND: Ground floor. Dirt floor?

MR. WALKER: Yeah, ground floor.

MR. AWAKUNI-SWETLAND: What held the roof up?

MR. WALKER: Well, there was a big pole right in the middle.

MR. AWAKUNI-SWETLAND: Was it like a tree or was it lumber, timber?

MR. WALKER: Oh, it was a log.

MR. AWAKUNI-SWETLAND: A log?

MR. WALKER: A big log. But, of course, I think it's built up with two-by-fours, you know, like that. Now, that's what happens, them two-by-fours gave way and that pole didn't do any good.

MR. AWAKUNI-SWETLAND: The ruins that are up north, here. There's a chimney — a brick chimney going up pretty much near the middle part of that roof. Do you remember that chimney?

MR. WALKER: Oh, it's kind of a — well, what should I say, a dog house. But it was built square. And anyway, them boards were nailed like that for ventilation.

MR. AWAKUNI-SWETLAND: Sure. I think this picture shows, from a different house. Like that?

MR. WALKER: Yeah, there you are. There you go.

MR. AWAKUNI-SWETLAND: Like a cupola, or something. Yeah, these are the open windows or louvers or something.

MR. WALKER: Yeah, there you go right there. There's your windows. This was a house up by —

MR. AWAKUNI-SWETLAND: This one is supposed to be over here east, Silas Woods, this one. But the one up north was similar?

MR. WALKER: Practically the same.

MR. AWAKUNI-SWETLAND: Do you remember a flag pole or anything up north?

MR. WALKER: No, I don't think so. If it did, I didn't know about it. I lived there since Silas Wood's... His house was right over in here.

MR. AWAKUNI-SWETLAND: I think the people were saying this picture of Silas Woods' place is — you're looking back west. This is — You know, Macy is on the other side of this hill.

MR. WALKER: Yeah, looking east.

MR. AWAKUNI-SWETLAND: You're looking east? So, you're standing on the ridge by Macy, looking towards the river?

MR. WALKER: Yeah.

MR. AWAKUNI-SWETLAND: Here's a barn and a shed.

MR. WALKER: Yeah.

MR. AWAKUNI-SWETLAND: A corn crib, or something. And you said that there was a racetrack down here?

MR. WALKER: The racetrack is over in here.

MR. AWAKUNI-SWETLAND: On the left side?

MR. WALKER: Yeah. And this was 40 acres and they had — they camped all along here like that. Up here on the hillside they had kind of a — well, sheds — low sheds. they had an exhibit for — like fairgrounds. They put their stuff in there and — I remember one time they had a pow wow there. And some way some how, a couple of white guys went broke and they asked the committee if they could put up a tent and put up a show there. They had a bear — a great big monster. And that other guy, he would wrestle that bear. Of course, you had to —

MR. AWAKUNI-SWETLAND: Pay to see it?

MR. WALKER: Yeah.

Talking about lands further east of Macy, towards the Missouri River...

MR. WALKER: That's the Miller place. That would be on the road going straight east.

MR. AWAKUNI-SWETLAND: Straight east?

MR. WALKER: Yeah. Of course, there was some houses built there. And Tom Miller, he lived down there and he farmed down there. And the same with Amos Lamson, And, what's his name, Brownrigg , John Brownrigg, they all lived down there. When I was on the council, this was all timber. So, the council, Alfred Gilpin, he was the Chairman, he decided to clear off all that timber and make farm ground out of it. After that, they kicked me off the council. They issued out army tents, big square tents. Every one of them got tents. They all just spread out like this and put up their tent and lived out there. Well, now, you see these project homes. Now they've built these project homes down that way, too.

MR. AWAKUNI-SWETLAND: Yeah, all along this road here and along this road, here and all the way out to here [east and north of Macy].

MR. WALKER: Yeah, way down there.

MR. AWAKUNI-SWETLAND: Was it you that mentioned to me last time we were talking about how the military used to camp over and shoot — you know, use target practice? [Looking at the Silas Woods picture]

MR. WALKER: Yeah, about right out this way, where it's kind of high. Of course, now, you go by that place and it's all trees, now. Just as you cross that first bridge. Back in there, that's where they had that camp. And I don't know, I think they must have target practice, or something, before it was all pasturage. You'd find those shells.

MR. AWAKUNI-SWETLAND: Yeah, the casings — the brass casings.

Looking South of Macy...

If you went south, I've heard that if you crossed Blackbird Creek going south — here's the post office and Lawrence and Kathryn Gilpin's place. If you go across Blackbird Creek, just here — this road going here, this is Matthew Tyndall's allotment here.

MR. WALKER: Yeah.

MR. AWAKUNI-SWETLAND: Was there — Do you remember a lodge being down there?

MR. WALKER: Yeah. See, that's right, uh-huh, yeah, back in the corner.

MR. AWAKUNI-SWETLAND: Close up to — Here's — There's trees here, so this is all farmland here in front —fields. But this green is where there's trees now. And there's a creek that runs — that blue line is the creek. Did that have a name or —

MR. WALKER: I don't remember.

MR. AWAKUNI-SWETLAND: Who would have used it?

MR. WALKER: Well, that old man, Matthew, I know him. He was a fussy old man. And he had one of those dagger pouch. Just like your eye glass case.

MR. AWAKUNI-SWETLAND: Okay, yeah.

MR. WALKER: Just like that. And the maybe he'd have about four or five butcher knives in there. He'd wear it on his belt. He never harmed anybody, but that's the way he was. Of course, he was a pretty crabby old man. His Indian name was *Masi*. That's how come Macy got its name. *Masi*, that "A" was an "ah." And Maryott — George Maryott, of course, he's another guy that was on the reservation. He's the one that got all the Indian land. He is the one that changed the name. Instead of that short "A," he made it a long "A." That's how come they made it Macy.

MR. AWAKUNI-SWETLAND: George Maryott, isn't he the one that had a trading post and a store, or something like that? Maryott City, they said, up there by Skunk Hollow Road somewhere.

MR. WALKER: Oh, a grocery store.

MR. AWAKUNI-SWETLAND: A grocery store.

MR. WALKER: That's that guy I was telling you about, George Maryott.

MR. AWAKUNI-SWETLAND: George Maryott.

MR. WALKER: He's the one. It's right in the middle of the road he had that store there and there was a road on both sides.

MR. AWAKUNI-SWETLAND: This house that was on the Tyndall place, did Matthew build it or was it already there?

MR. AWAKUNI-SWETLAND: I don't know about that. But there's a lot of the original houses. Some of them are still standing there.

MR. AWAKUNI-SWETLAND: And the lodge, the dance lodge, was it a circular lodge that he had down there?

MR. WALKER: It's a lodge, a round lodge.

MR. AWAKUNI-SWETLAND: A round lodge?

MR. WALKER: Yeah.

MR. AWAKUNI-SWETLAND: Kind of like this other one?

MR. WALKER: Uh-huh.

MR. AWAKUNI-SWETLAND: What might have happened to it?

MR. WALKER: Well, I don't know how they done away with it, I don't know. Of course, that might have happened while I was out.

MR. AWAKUNI-SWETLAND: Who might know about that lodge down there?

MR. WALKER: I don't know. Practically all the old families are gone. You might talk to Dennis Turner. His dad, John Turner and Henry Turner is the old man. John Turner is the son. And Dennis is the grandson. Them guys, they are pretty well — they are pretty well learned. That is, Henry, the old man Henry, he's pretty well posted on things. And it might be that he might have, you know, in everyday conversation, you know, might have heard some things. So, he'd be the one. Yeah, I think he would be the only one. Right at the present time I think he's the treasurer of the tribal council.

The traveling dance lodge...

MR. AWAKUNI-SWETLAND: Okay. The house that you were talking about, the first time we started talking about houses, the one that got moved a couple of times, or whatever and finally was burned down, what's the whole story on that?

MR. WALKER: Well, that — To begin with, that was the lodge close to that Hiram Mitchell's [place]. Quite a prominent man. Sort of an outstanding man. He took to having that Peyote Society. He was living on the place, the house, the farm. A few of those members of that society got together and built that lodge. It was a sacred lodge. When they built that lodge, they built that fireplace right in the middle. And it's concrete.

MR. AWAKUNI-SWETLAND: Concrete, in the middle of the floor.

MR. WALKER: And the fireplace. And right at the end of that, where the half-moon shape comes out, they built a round kind of a ball, like — half of a ball, only it's flat. Then they marked that cross on there. They was going good. Everybody was — It was going good. They were all religious. They would intend to have a meeting and everybody would come. They would have their meetings and ceremonies and sometimes — I believe, I don't know, they might have had hand games there, too. But this other organization, my in-law, Bert Freemont — I forget his brother's name. We called him *Shiⁿha*. Bert was *gakuwiⁿxe* [agitated]. They're all *xube* [sacred]. And of course, they had some followers...

MR. AWAKUNI-SWETLAND: It started at Hiram Mitchell's place, though?

MR. WALKER: Yeah, that was the start. They started from there. But their idea was, well, sort of an Indian church.

MR. AWAKUNI-SWETLAND: Yeah, like the Native American church. But Bert Fremont —

MR. WALKER: Paul and, like, they're all gone, now. I forget, but anyway, they all went in on it. Of course, some of them they had powwow time. They had their marble dance. But that's how they — that bunch took that barn and moved it to another place.

MR. AWAKUNI-SWETLAND: They moved it further down south.

MR. WALKER: Further west.

MR. AWAKUNI-SWETLAND: Let's see, maybe we can find out where [consulting topographic maps].

MR. WALKER: Pete Blackbird took it down there. Pete Blackbird's place. The creek kinda runs kind of like that and the lodge was built right there, right where it's flat. So, that's the Blackbird Creek.

MR. AWAKUNI-SWETLAND: It's on Blackbird Creek. Well, here's Blackbird Creek from Macy down south [consulting the 1882 allotment map]. Pete Blackbird had an allotment right here just south of Macy, one. And then he had another one — I'd have to look up where that number is. Those are the numbers for the allotments. If we go out driving around, would you be able to point out where that lodge started and where it ended? Would we be able to find those sites?

MR. WALKER: Yeah.

MR. AWAKUNI-SWETLAND: You could remember that? Okay.

MR. WALKER: One place — that place, but the lodge that we're talking about now, the one they moved on Pete Blackbird's place, might have to go through some pretty rough roads.

MR. AWAKUNI-SWETLAND: Well, if there's a road, we'll go on it. We might have to walk back, but —

MR. WALKER: That's it.

MR. AWAKUNI-SWETLAND: But, we can try and track it down.

So, they moved it and that's where they were having their Pebble Society dances and Shell [Society], and all of that stuff? How long did that last?

MR. WALKER: Well, I don't think it lasted very long. Because, like I say, I wasn't here. And during that time they could have moved it. That same lodge, they moved it just further back south. I could show you the place to where that lodge moved back. I could show you that place. That's that road going to Genevieve's [Robinson]. You go straight west and over the hill and the lodge was built like that.

MR. AWAKUNI-SWETLAND: And what happened to it in the end?

MR. WALKER: Well, I don't know what happened after that. I suppose they tore it down. But anyway, when they moved it back, I think the Young Skunks, *Mo^{n}gazhi^{n}ga*, I think they took charge. They had their war dances, hand games, and like that.

MR. AWAKUNI-SWETLAND: Do you remember who was in the Young Skunks?

MR. WALKER: The Baxters. The Baxter brothers. Fred Baxter, Frank Baxter and his brother, Vic. And a few others like Bert Freemont's in-law, Walt Peabody. This old man over here, Charlie Edwards. He was one of them, too. He was one of the Young Skunks. Of course quite a few of them died off, too. Well, in fact, they're all gone. Just the children, their offspring are left.

Say, you could to talk to Zac Drum. His dad, Pete Drum. He was one of them that was in that *Mo^{n}gazhi^{n}ga*. It might be that he can tell you something, too.

MR. AWAKUNI-SWETLAND: The *Mo^{n}gazhi^{n}ga* were different from the Old Skunk Lodge, true?

MR. WALKER: The *Mo^{n}ga*. Yeah, they're different.

MR. AWAKUNI-SWETLAND: They are a different organization?

MR. WALKER: Different.

MR. AWAKUNI-SWETLAND: Can you remember some of the folks that belonged to the *Mo^{n}ga*?

MR. WALKER: I don't know. Well, they are all gone, now. I don't know.

MR. AWAKUNI-SWETLAND: Where did the Gilpins fit in? Joe Gilpin, who lives down in Omaha, now, old man Joe, about 70-some years old. He was talking about the Old Skunk Lodge. So, would his folks have been in that one? Not the Little Skunks but the — They talk about one over by Paul Thomas' place. They talk about Warren Davis. Which one was that?

MR. WALKER: Paul Thomas, that's — Paul Thomas lived up on the hill and it's just right below that is where the Tyndall Lodge was.

MR. AWAKUNI-SWETLAND: The Matthew Tyndall Lodge. Paul Thomas, number 412, [consulting the 1882 allotment map]. See, here's Macy, just south is number 412, that's the 40 acres that Paul Thomas had. Here's Matthew Tyndall's place. So, we're talking about the Matthew Tyndall house?

MR. WALKER: Yeah. Here's the lodge and it would be right about in that corner there.

MR. AWAKUNI-SWETLAND: Okay. On the east side or west side of that creek?

MR. WALKER: Southeast corner.

MR. AWAKUNI-SWETLAND: Southeast. Okay. They talk about another lodge that Warren Davis was somehow associated with. Warren Davis had an allotment down here, south, coming across the second bridge. Come down another couple of miles.

MR. WALKER: That's that place that I said I could show you.

MR. AWAKUNI-SWETLAND: That's the one you'd be able to — Okay, great. And this is the one that they were moving around different places?
MR. WALKER: Yeah. They moved it three times, I think.

MR. AWAKUNI-SWETLAND: Three times?

MR. WALKER: Yeah.

MR. AWAKUNI-SWETLAND: They moved it from Hiram Mitchell's place.

MR. WALKER: Then over at Blackbird.

MR. AWAKUNI-SWETLAND: To Pete Blackbird's place.

MR. WALKER: And then back down the —

MR. AWAKUNI-SWETLAND: Then over here near the Warren Davis place?

MR. WALKER: Yeah.

MR. AWAKUNI-SWETLAND: Okay. Great. And the Old Skunk —

MR. WALKER: I don't know where that is.

MR. AWAKUNI-SWETLAND: And the Little Skunk, they must have been further south?

MR. WALKER: Well, they're the ones that were further south — down here by —

MR. AWAKUNI-SWETLAND: No. Here's the —

MR. WALKER: — Warren Davis.

MR. AWAKUNI-SWETLAND: Warren Davis, that's one of the skunks?

MR. WALKER: That's the Young Skunk.

MR. AWAKUNI-SWETLAND: Okay. *Mo^{n}gazhi^{n}ga*. So, they went from Hiram Mitchell to Pete Blackbird to Warren Davis and that's where the Little Skunk's name come in?

MR. WALKER: Yeah, that's — after its kinda idle and the Young Skunk come in.

MR. AWAKUNI-SWETLAND: Okay. Let's see. And if we go over towards where this is [East of Macy], Silas Woods' place, you'd be able to probably point out right about where everything was, huh? The racetrack, the lodge, his house? Great.

MR. WALKER: I think that where that lodge is, that house, barn and stuff, I think that's the original place. I think that's the original [allotment era] house. I think I'm pretty sure, now. Yeah, I believe so.

MR. AWAKUNI-SWETLAND: We'll go take a look at it. We'll take what pictures we have and take a peek at it.

Lodges West of Macy...

Let's see, here's Macy and we come out and go across Blackbird Creek and Macy is sitting right here. We come out, we cross the creek, come to that first four corners and continue up the hill and down the hill. Here's the old Robinson place and that's that little creek in there. Right here, that little white area, that's where that aerial photo shows the Wind Lodge to be sitting.

MR. WALKER: Yeah. Then that Lyons place is up here. Harry Lyons, his house.

MR. AWAKUNI-SWETLAND: OH, that's where Harry Lyons was?

MR. WALKER: Yeah.

MR. AWAKUNI-SWETLAND: Everybody is always talking about there was a house they called the Horseshoe House Lodge, because Harry — it was near Harry Lyons. It was in a horseshoe bend. Well, that's a horseshoe bend [on the map]. That creek makes a horseshoe. Here, I was confusing it as a whole different lodge. It's the same one.

MR. WALKER: Uh-huh.

MR. AWAKUNI-SWETLAND: So, Harry Lyons was on the north side?

MR. WALKER: Yeah, that house and then the barns sat further back.

MR. AWAKUNI-SWETLAND: Where did the McCauley's have their —
Didn't the McCauley's live over — Eva McCauley was talking about having to carry water across the road.

MR. WALKER: Oh, that's — Jim McCauley, inter-married into that family and I think he — he lived with — Jim Lyons' wife. She died, see, and he
married that old lady. That's how come — you know, you mentioned her
name and that guy that drums, *xuka*...

MR. AWAKUNI-SWETLAND: Mike, that's her son.

MR. WALKER: Well, that's Jim McCauley's son and daughter.

MR. AWAKUNI-SWETLAND: Okay.

MR. WALKER: So, if McCauley's slapping their name on that, why * * *

MR. AWAKUNI-SWETLAND: It's Lyons up there, then?

MR. WALKER: It's Lyons' lodge. They're the one that call themselves
Sisabe [Black Foot].

MR. AWAKUNI-SWETLAND: Didn't the *Sisabe* get together out at old
Ted White, Sr.'s place? That would be just over here, you know, north.
Instead of coming up over the hill, you cross the bridge, Blackbird Creek
west to Macy, come to Four Corners, you turn north and you go around
that corner. And Ted White's place was up here somewhere.

MR. WALKER: I really don't know where he lived. But then, Aunt Mariah,
she — that road going west and there's another road that comes in this way.
And kind of a ditch right here. And a small bridge. And Aunt Mariah —
and, of course, there's some trees right in here, and a road that turns in
there. And behind them trees, that's where Aunt Mariah lived.

MR. AWAKUNI-SWETLAND: Mariah?.

MR. WALKER: Mariah. I think that's Ted's mother.

MR. AWAKUNI-SWETLAND: Okay. Florence White Grant, she was talking about from where the Wind Lodge was standing, across the creek there,

on the south side there was a little one-room house. Old Lady Julia Sheradin — Julia White lived there.

MR. WALKER: I think that's the one — that's the one.

MR. AWAKUNI-SWETLAND: That's the one?

MR. WALKER: That's the one. I've got it wrong there. North — what White told you, I think he's right.

MR. AWAKUNI-SWETLAND: There's a little one-room house here. Julia White lived there. And up on this side hill, here, coming up to this road, it's all hay meadow now, [there was a] powwow grounds. They used to — Some guy named Cayou had a merry-go-round and they came out and they danced here. It would be just west of that Wind Lodge. They said there was a powwow grounds here. Does that ring any bells?

MR. WALKER: Lee, Lee Cayou. Yeah, he used to run that steam merry-go-round.

MR. AWAKUNI-SWETLAND: A steam one. What years would that be, 1920s, '30s, '40s?

MR. WALKER: Oh, I was small, so it would be way back there somewhere. Ted White's mother, she's in my clan [*Tesi^{n}de^n*]. Well, Ted is too.

MR. AWAKUNI-SWETLAND: Rufus White is pretty young, isn't he?

MR. WALKER: Yeah, he's one of them. I think there's one younger than him. I think he's — I don't know just where he is now. But anyway, he was down in Omaha for a while at a street crossing, a car ran over him and kind of crippled. Theodore.

MR. AWAKUNI-SWETLAND: Ted, Jr. — Theodore, Jr.

MR. WALKER: And my next door neighbor here, I think he's the oldest of the boys. Joe White.

MR. AWAKUNI-SWETLAND: Joe. I'll ask him about his folks' place.

MR. WALKER: He's got his own place down west of Macy here.

END TAPE

Appendix C
RAMONA TURNER GREANY
June 24, 1992

Ramona Turner was born in the early part of the twentieth century. She is the daughter of Henry Turner, and the Granddaughter of Little Chief (Oliver Turner), a prominent Omaha leader of the nineteenth century. In the 1990s Ramona was residing in an allotment-era house on the bluff overlooking the Missouri River bottomland. Horse Head Creek runs in front of her house on the south side, and the Horse Head Lodge was built on the adjoining land to the west of her home. Through the Omaha kinship system Ramona was my Grandmother. We had had occasional opportunities to visit prior to the dance lodge project.

Ramona was asked to participate in the dance lodge project due to her family's history of lodge membership, her past and current proximity to the Horse Head Lodge structure, and her publicly recognized status as an elder with a traditionalist's devotion to cultural preservation and transmission. Ramona had become active in sweat lodge and sun dance practices, and was in the process of packing for a trip to ceremonies in South Dakota when I arrived for an interview. Ramona was interviewed in her rural home along Horse Head Creek, north of Macy, Nebraska.

Talking about the Mark of Honor...

MS. GREANY: Well, just a few things I could probably answer your questions, but I can't give you the whole information, because I probably don't know. [Perhaps] somebody older than me. But one of my full sisters said, "Well, I've lived here all my life in this house, here." And I know what they used to talk about. They used to say that.

There were several people that gave that Mark of Honor tattoos [in] the sacred way. And it was two people who go by the way of *Mo^{n}shti^{n}ga* —

Grandma Mable Hamilton told me, he's the one who gave her that. And my mother was that way, too.

But that old man Silas Wood, I guess he came in towards the last.

And since that old man [Silas] is dead, nobody never mentioned that Mark of Honor, until later. I mean, nobody has tried to revive it or anything like that. We thought about reviving it, but we would have to go into something deeper. There was a whole lot to it. There were songs to that. I forgot what they call it... *Ho^nhewachi.* It was the Blessed Night Society, I think they said.

And you had to be chief's daughter or chief's off-spring, like the oldest one, they say. My mother was one. And my Aunt Clemma, Old Man Little Chief. Aunt Clemma was Old Man Little Chief's daughter, did you know that? Lenna and them is my own blood. Old Man Little Chief. He is the father of my father and Aunt Minnie Solomon. Minnie, Georgene's mother, Elizabeth's mother — Elizabeth Saunsoci. Okay? And here this old man had Aunt Clemma. Clemma Saunsoci, She went by [the name] Mitchell.

MR. AWAKUNI-SWETLAND: Oh, that's why I didn't hear of her.

MS. GREANY: You see. Because Elizabeth probably didn't know. Elizabeth moved away long before — way — they went to Lincoln long time. And maybe she forgot. Maybe Aunt Minnie didn't tell her. Or, maybe she knew it and just didn't think nothing and maybe she thought everybody knew it. But then when my father died, Aunt Clemma was sitting right here, and she told me that. She said, "I'm your aunt," she said. "Your father is my brother," she said. "Old Man Little Chief is my father. He gave me this. *Xthexthe o^nkitha,*" she said. "He done this Mark of Honor. He took me. I'm his oldest daughter," she said. "So," she said, "you're mine." And "*wiwita ni*" she said, "*Thiadi,* your father is my brother," she said.

And that's what she told me, Aunt Clemma did. And my father said that. He said, "Old Man [Little Chief] claimed her." And he even gave her a little house down here. There was a house — That house was taken up there where that old place is. That old place where Elizabeth's mother lived — Aunt Clemma lived.

Talking about Dance Lodges, the Shell Society, medicine bundles...

MR. AWAKUNI-SWETLAND: It was actually my adopted Omaha Grandmother Elizabeth Saunsoci Stabler that started me on this Dance Lodge project. Because you know the old Harry Solomon house out there, west of Macy? Across the road from Joe Field's place? They would stay there when they come up [from Lincoln] for dances or something, on weekends. They'd camp out there — sleep out there. And we'd always drive that old road coming in from the west. There was a little creek down there and you'd cross over it. And Grandma Elizabeth would always point off to that south side of the road. She said, "Right there used to be the Wind Lodge."

MS. GREANY: Yeah, it's west of here, over that hill. Right there. It's over the hill and where Lyons — Harry Lyons lived. There was a house there and that Wind Lodge was right there. And I remember there was even a pump there — water in that Wind Lodge. Because the people used to say, "They're going to have a dance tonight." My dad used to dance. *Hethushka* [War Dance], you know. He danced. That was his life, like, you know. He used to really take interest in it. Fixing his regalia and everything. He used to go dancing. And my mother used to dance, too, you know. They really went in for that, in them days. We used to go in horse — in a team. I remember that lodge was there.

I don't know if they [held] *xube wathate* [sacred feast] there. I don't think so. I know they did over here. They did over there at that Little Warrior's [Lodge] — that last — that society, I think it was Marble Society had their ceremony there. My father went in, and I went in with him. I was a little girl. That's the last one I remember.

MR. AWAKUNI-SWETLAND: Where was that at?

MS. GREANY: Gilbert Morris's place right there.

MR. AWAKUNI-SWETLAND: Okay, just north of Macy right? — okay.

MS. GREANY: Yeah. They had it right there in a real nice place, you know, [with a] real kind of shade. I don't know who built that, either. I don't know that part. Somebody must know. But, anyway, they used to have their dances there. And I remember they had that society, you know, dance. And my father was invited and they had to take their wooden bowls and they have the special bowls — wooden bowls that were sacred. They used the pipe. They used all sacred things. And that's when I found out this Shell Society had one clan that Old Man — I mean Charlie Stabler was in it, his clan.

MR. AWAKUNI-SWETLAND: I^nkesabe?

MS. GREANY: Un-huh, Buffalo Clan. Buffalo Clan, this man was — he was a *wagaxtho^n* [ritual servant]. He was the one, The one [who] can go in the center [of the lodge] and wait on people, whatever, light their pipes and fix the fire and fix the things, you know — go around. And he was — It seemed like he was the only one. And now they are still carrying it [on], like brother John Turner, and them, they carried it, [including] Lambert. They said *I^nkesabe* had the right to cut the cake because they come from there, you see, the *wagaxtho^n*. But they are the ones that can do that, they said. If there's no *I^nkesabe* women, a man can mark it — mark that cake and then they get somebody to cut it for them.

So, I remember that part they talked about. Because there was one guy named John McCauley. "John Hay," they called him. He was a *nudo^n- ho^nga* [leader] in that way. Because my grandfather — My people were medicine people. My grandfather, Little Chief and Old Man Jacob Parker, we were all one family. Jacob Parker's sister was my grandfather's mother. We come in like that. I'm closely related to Emily Parker. Her and I are the only ones living that has these bundles... *Washishka* [Shell Society] bundles of medicines and things. Her and I are the only ones, and we're still living. It was such a secret sacred society of the Omaha Tribe. It's always a secret. Lillian Wolf was saying that the other day. She doesn't want to give information out. "Well, why are we going to give away our information?" she said. "Because," she said, "they're going to write it down and make money on it," she said.

MR. AWAKUNI-SWETLAND: People blamed me of wanting to do the same thing [with this Dance Lodge project]. And I said, "What gets done with this information here is up to the tribe to decide. It's up to the elderly folks."

MS. GREANY: Well, someday if you've got it written down, well maybe it might go down that the generations will know. Somebody wrote something down for generations. The kids will say, "Well, our Omaha people, I guess they had lodges," you know. That's to be seen. That's further – [in the] future. I think about that. I always think about these things, you know, but [there is] nobody to talk to. Nobody to tell. In *Umo^nho^n* way, you brought things [traditional food offerings]. That's when I could talk to you. Otherwise, I can't. I'm not supposed to.

MR. AWAKUNI-SWETLAND: That's why, when we were talking in the tribal council building the other day, you kind of stopped and said, "Oh, I'm giving things away." And that's right, you were right. It's inappropriate for me and you to have a conversation out in public like that. If I want to know something, I need to sacrifice, come over here and ask you, at your house. That's how Grandpa Charlie [Stabler] raised me. He said, "Take the time. Go over there. Talk to that person."

MS. GREANY: Yes. And the lodge, this lodge over here, I remember as soon as you enter that door, right to the side here was a table, like, against the wall. And somebody built boards on there. It was a table with legs on there like that. They put the food on there. And they had a fireplace right there. They had a great big kettle, I remember, they cooked the food in that. And some men are watching it and women — somebody. And then that place was big enough where the singers sat right in the middle, on the ground. And we all carried blankets. We carried — Our mothers used to fix out of overalls or kind of thick material, they make a quilt. Kind of make it thick and then that's what we used to sit on. Each home had them, just like rugs.

We had those and we had them for Native American Church, too. We've had them — Instead of now you can buy rugs, remnants-like, you know. You can roll them and have them. But them days we had to make quilts. Long strips like. Then we put them around. People bring their own. Some of them had horse hide.

MR. AWAKUNI-SWETLAND: Horse hide?

MS. GREANY: Horse hide or cow hide — Because I know we had one.

MR. AWAKUNI-SWETLAND: With the hair still on it?

MS. GREANY: Uh-huh, with the hair still on there and it was lined. It had a lining. Maybe they had them made. But we used to use them when we would go in our lumber wagon and we'd cover up. And they'd be just warm, you know. We couldn't feel that cold air. They'd have straw in that wagon.

And my father used to have real good horses that he fed them good. He took care of his horses all the time, and watered them, fed them corn. He had real pretty horses and we used to go to town in that. And my mother made some quilts, like, you know, that cushion like. We used to go in the wagon and it would be warm. I remember that, you know.

MR. AWAKUNI-SWETLAND: Did you go to these dances in the winter time?

MS. GREANY: In the winter time, yes. They had a hot fire going. People took their blankets in there and they sat on the ground. They'd make, maybe, two rows, sitting on the ground. Right in the center, then they danced. And then when they're going to dance the war dance, well the women took their blankets and put them back, you know.

They had a little bench — Later I found out they had a little bench made again — all the way around, seated — one seat, like all the way around inside where people could sit. But some of them sat on the ground. Old people sit on the ground and some sit on the bench. And it was kind of a wide board like that [indicating a width with her hands].

MR. AWAKUNI-SWETLAND: About 12 inches?

MS. GREANY: Uh-huh. And they'd fix that all the way around. It was like that over here, [at] Horse Head. And I remember in 1954 that was the last time I went over here. And I was married to John GREANY. We got married legally. He was a Southern Cheyenne. And we got married and here they had this dance over here, so we walked over there. Him and I, we walked across this field. There was a road over there. We went over there and we got over there and I remember I had a blanket and I just sat on the ground and John, he — I forgot where he sat. Anyway, I think on that bench. And here somebody — they had adoption here. They adopted him, Suzette Turner, Suzette La Flesche.

MR. AWAKUNI-SWETLAND: Your Sister-in-Law?

MS. GREANY: She adopted John GREANY, my husband, for brother, right there. And people just recognized him and just shook hands with him and just — you know, things like that. They used to do things like that, you know. And dances –i t seemed like there were groups, northern *xekugthi* they called them this side. I don't know how you pronounce that in English, but it's up here.

And *Mo^{n}ga* — little skunks down there [south of Macy]. *Mo^{n}ga*, skunk. They said, "*Mo^{n}ga ti*," that was Skunk Lodge —

And then out there [west of Macy] was Wind — Wind Lodge. *Tade ti*, "*Tade*," they said,.

Then this one over here [north of Macy, south of Horse Head Lodge] was Little Warrior — *Hethushka zhi^{n}ga*.

I remember them four lodges. I remember, when we used to go — we used to think we were going way down south, you know, because they were southern — the southern Indians lived over there, you know, and we used to kind of go visit. They used to say, "The northern people are here to visit," you know, like that. They used to give away to each other. They used to be good to one another, you know, invite each other. Them things are — That's traditional in culture, you know. I know a lot of things. I've lived here all my life. Some of us, we know. Some of us that's lived here, never left, we still know what our people used to do. But the younger people now, they don't know and they don't know — they don't understand, even our language. Our younger people don't understand our language.

Today [at a funeral for an elder Omaha] the [Omaha Tribal] chairman [Doran Morris] was saying that. He said, "It's too bad we're losing our language," he said. "My [deceased] grandma, here, sure talked good Indian." And Aunt Lucille Gilpin, she was good — you know, she talked real good Indian. He said "We're losing that." He said, "I don't think our children talk that language, either." So, he was talking about that today

So, today that's all I know about them lodges.

MR. AWAKUNI-SWETLAND: When you went into the Horse Head Lodge over here [on the land west of Ramona's house], you're talking about a fireplace to the right side of the doorway.

MS. GREANY: As you enter, uh-huh.

MR. AWAKUNI-SWETLAND: Where was the — any other fire? How did they keep it warm besides that one fire? Was there any other fireplace in there?

MS. GREANY: Let's see.

MR. AWAKUNI-SWETLAND: Because I'm thinking of that chimney that's sticking up.

MS. GREANY: Yeah, they had a stove in there. A big old stove.

MR. AWAKUNI-SWETLAND: Was it in the middle of off to the side.

MS. GREANY: I think it was off to the side, because it was – them people used to really cut wood them days, you know. That was something everybody done.

MR. AWAKUNI-SWETLAND: There wasn't as much brush and stuff down here, was there?

MS. GREANY: It was clear. It was nice. And they had some posts hanging — you know, set aside for the horses, where they could tie their horses.

Teams, they had them there, too.

MR. AWAKUNI-SWETLAND: What time would people start gathering over there for a typical dance?

MS. GREANY: About evening. I suppose around — I think they ate supper after. I think they start cooking right away. Because I know, John and I went over there and that was the last time I saw that.

MR. AWAKUNI-SWETLAND: Were they eating after dark?

MS. GREANY: No. They didn't believe in that. Umo^nho^n didn't believe in that. If they do, they put out soup for the spirits. Soup, right before they ate they put out food so it would be all right. The spirits are fed. That's one thing they don't say today. They don't say that now. Louie Dick was talking today, and I know what he meant. He said, "You people stay here, respect the family. Stay here until they take the body out. And follow them up to the cemetery," he said. "Respect that body," he said. That's what the old people said. And people, him talking like that, some people don't like him, you know. They said he talks too much. But I agree with him, myself, because I know that's the way our people were. They had respect, they had love for each other, you know. Nobody never did — I never did see a fight or a quarrel or anything or say bad things to each other.

MR. AWAKUNI-SWETLAND: Did they ever use these lodges for funerals, for wakes or anything?

MS. GREANY: No, they took them at their own homes. When my father died, we had him here. When my Aunt Minnie died, we had her here, so people take their bodies in their own homes. But just recently they've been taking them to the building.

MR. AWAKUNI-SWETLAND: Where did the light come from for this lodge here? Where is the light? How did you have light inside?

MS. GREANY: I think they had gasoline — gas lamps, I think. They called that lantern *sho^{n}ge wano^{n}go^{n}gthe*. That means, horse, you know, like barn, a horse. "*Sho^{n}ge wano^{n}go^{n}gthe*," they say. They mean that lantern.

MR. AWAKUNI-SWETLAND: Kerosene?

MS. GREANY: Uh-huh, kerosene and that. And they had them, too.

MR. AWAKUNI-SWETLAND: Okay. And would they dance all night?

MS. GREANY: Yeah, they did. Because my father, when they danced war dance, I guess they got into it so — I guess it was just so — the spiritual power comes in, you know. Whatever the Indians do, this is working with the power. People don't know that. Maybe you know it when you dance. Do you get that real good feeling when you dance?

MR. AWAKUNI-SWETLAND: Yes. If I go up there and I'm feeling sick, if the singing is right and the people are right and I'm dancing, I get all well.

MS. GREANY: You get well, because that drum is sacred. It's a sacred drum, and then you get well. Now, that's the way they were, I guess.

And how that name, *Gtho^nthi^n to^nga*, "Big Crazy" came about. We used to have a group over here. Old Man Paul Lovejoy, he went to Carlisle. So, he was kind of educated. He talked good English. Good handwriting. That Old Man used to be the head of that Horse Head Lodge, I mean Big Crazy. And we used to all gather. My father was in that group, Joe Parker, Isaac Springer, Isaac Sherman, Charlie Walker, Bill Walker, Bill Lovejoy. This was all this group, here. We lived here. "*Xe kugthi*," they call it right here. *Xekugthi.* Come north of here, towards the river, you see. It's kind of a valley, like, right here. That's what they called us up here in this part.

They used to dance. That was in my father's days, when they danced all night, I guess. They had good time, they said. They [had] giveaways and everything. And there was this one man, I guess, he felt so good, just dancing so good, I guess he went outside and wanted to giveaway. He went outside and unhitched his horse, one side. He had a team of horses. He brought that horse in here [into the lodge]. And they said, "*Gtho^nthi^n to^nga*," they called him. The Big Crazy. He had that name and carried [it] on.

So, later on in years, well after — I think it was 1970 — anyway, John Turner and his wife got in there and they talked about the name, *Gtho^nthi^n to^nga*, Because some of them didn't like to be called *Gtho^nthi^n to^nga*. Pete Saunsoci, and them they used to sing. And Sarpy. They were good singers. And they said, "We'll call it Horse Head Lodge. *Sho^nge pa, Sho^nge pa*," they said. So, that's when the name [changed] — but still they say *Gtho^nthi^n to^nga*. And then I left. John and I moved to Omaha and we were gone. We used to come home on weekends, though. He worked down there. We kind of got away from the group and then others joined. Pretty soon, nobody — it's gone.

But I heard of, going towards the highway [75], along there Old Lady

Woods, Silas Woods lived over there. She belonged to the Shell Society, because my folks used to go over there. They never had dances, but they had feasts that was just only about six — five or six left. They couldn't have dances but they used to have feasts in the spring and fall, feasts. They'd all *xube wathate* [sacred feast] And there was just them — the family, they'd be singing. They'd sing them songs. Because I remember that. And it was at that house that Old Lady Woods — I forgot her English name — but she was one of the members. And I guess there must have been a lodge there, too, because they had powwows there.

END TAPE

Appendix D
GERTRUDE "EMILY" PARKER
July 02, 1992

Gertrude Parker was born in the early part of the twentieth century. She is the daughter of Charles Parker, who was widely recognized as the last Omaha person to be both knowledgeable and qualified to handle sacred objects and bundles. The original Horse Head Lodge was built on her grandfather Eli Parker's allotment. That lodge experienced various remodelings until its collapse in 1969. It provides the sole remaining physical evidence of dance lodge structures in 1992. Prior to, and since the death of her father, Gertrude has inherited the responsibilities related to the maintenance of the many sacred objects left in her father's care. Because of this status, she was asked to participate in the dance lodge project. It was considered appropriate to ask Gertrude for permission to enter the Parker family land in order to inspect the Horse Head Lodge ruins.

Prior to the dance lodge project I was not personally familiar with Gertrude. Tom C. Walker recommended that I speak with Gertrude, and volunteered to accompany me for introductions. I did not know which term of relationship to use. Tom C. made some calculations at our first meeting and suggested I call Gertrude "Niece", although I never fully comprehended the connections that permitted that term. Gertrude willingly agreed to our requests to inspect the Horse Head ruins, and we returned several times through the summer to her home for short visits. The following interview includes Tom C. Walker in Gertrude's rural home, south of Macy, Nebraska.

Horse Head Lodge...

MR. AWAKUNI-SWETLAND: You said that you knew about the Horse Head lodge the most. Can you describe it? The shape... what shape would it be like? What would you see when you went in?

MS. PARKER: The shape was round. The door was on the east. When we get there late. There were people in there already seated and ready for the celebration, whatever they were going to have. Other than that I don't believe there was anybody there. It was vacant. Just on celebrations. Then it was open to the public.

MR. AWAKUNI-SWETLAND: What kind of activities did they have over there?

MS. PARKER: They had activities, always for everybody.

They had hand game, only, sometimes. And they had war dance and they had birthday parties.

Holidays like Christmas, Thanksgiving, they'd have big celebration.

Giveaways to one another.

I never went that much because I was a younger age. But I'm sure my parents went.

MR. WALKER to AWAKUNI-SWETLAND: *xube wachigaxe*. Marble Dance?

MR. AWAKUNI-SWETLAND: *xube wachigaxe a?* Did they every have that Marble Dance up there [he said]?

MS. PARKER: I think they did. I'm not quite sure. I think they did. They most generally always had that east of Macy. I remember Silas Wood, that old place there, they always had it. I don't think they had anything. If it was sacred, at times, I never got to go because you're not supposed to go in there anyway. Only the one's that belonged in there. He never took us. Dad never took us there. But if it was an activity for everyone to enjoy, then he would take us.

So that was what I was telling you. I don't want to tell you anything that I never saw or never been to. But I did go to those.

MR. AWAKUNI-SWETLAND: Okay. That's good that you won't make up anything. That's good.

MS. PARKER: That's what my dad told me. He said that [if] you don't know what they ask you — something like that. If you don't know, you don't tell them something that you don't know. Just tell them the truth. It's better that way. Because they can't come back on you. Where something you told wasn't true. So it's like I'm telling you now. We never went to those sacred places. He went. Whether he belonged in there, I wouldn't know that.

MR. AWAKUNI-SWETLAND: You were showing me that picture that Wade [Miller] painted. You said there was a stove just inside that doorway. Let's see if the doorway is facing East. You go in, it's on that right hand side on that corner. I heard people talk about there's certain places kind of honor seats, and this and that. Where would people be sitting. Where would certain people sit?

MS. PARKER: It all depended on who belonged in that... they called it the Big Crazies. They always on the north side. And on the south side was open to the public.

MR. AWAKUNI-SWETLAND: Where did the *nudo^{n}ho^{n}ga*, whoever was in charge of that activity, where did they sit?

MS. PARKER: About in the center facing east and the drum was always in the center. And the singers.

MR. AWAKUNI-SWETLAND: Where was that chimney that is standing there.

MS. PARKER: In the center.

MR. AWAKUNI-SWETLAND: So let me draw a circle: Here's east, the doorway and that stove you said was over on this side.

MS. PARKER: Yeah, Not close to the wall.

MR. AWAKUNI-SWETLAND: Not close to the wall - more over here?

MS. PARKER: Yeah, and the chimney was right here.

MR. AWAKUNI-SWETLAND: And the singers?

MS. PARKER: Right around in here.

MR. AWAKUNI-SWETLAND: Right here?

MS. PARKER: uh-hum.

MR. AWAKUNI-SWETLAND: The leaders, who ever's in charge?

MS. PARKER: Okay

MR. AWAKUNI-SWETLAND: Northside would be this side.

MS. PARKER: Uh-hum.

MR. AWAKUNI-SWETLAND: So this is north side and this is south side. Did you have somebody sitting at the door?

MS. PARKER: No. I don't remember. Maybe if somebody got unruly. Other than that...

MR. AWAKUNI-SWETLAND: And the people sat on the ground?

MS. PARKER: Uh-hum.

MR. AWAKUNI-SWETLAND: Do you remember any benches or anything?

MS. PARKER: Later. They were back here [indicating along the wall].

MR. AWAKUNI-SWETLAND: If you walked in... What held the roof up?

MS. PARKER: Poles.

MR. AWAKUNI-SWETLAND: There were poles?

MS. PARKER: Uh-hum.

MR. AWAKUNI-SWETLAND: Where were the poles at?

MS. PARKER: Around there [indicating the center of the lodge floor area]. This [the chimney] was built in the center. Them poles was about like that [indicating a 12-18 inch circumference with her hands].

MR. AWAKUNI-SWETLAND: Do you remember how many poles?

MS. PARKER: It was about that big around. There was four probably.

MR. AWAKUNI-SWETLAND: And they were around the chimney?

MS. PARKER: Uhhum.

MR. AWAKUNI-SWETLAND to MR. WALKER: That one pole that we saw on the ground?

MR. WALKER: Uh-hum.

MR. AWAKUNI-SWETLAND to MR. WALKER: That would be about the right size.

MR. AWAKUNI-SWETLAND to MS. PARKER: There's one pole that's still up there. It's on the ground. But it's about that big around [indicating a 12-18 inch circumference with my hands].

MS. PARKER: That's what it was. Four of them, though. Where'd they got them [from]? If you had asked me - I should have known. But I never did question that. Ask him where'd they gotten certain things. I just barely remember now that he said something about that door.

MR. AWAKUNI-SWETLAND: uh-hum

MS. PARKER: What did you said it had on?

MR. AWAKUNI-SWETLAND: Two horses heads.

MS. PARKER: uh-hum. I can barely remember him saying something about that. That what I said that I should have got something like this [indicating the tape recorder] and wrote it all down. Maybe today it'd be good history.

MR. AWAKUNI-SWETLAND: Imagine you've just walked inside that door and those posts and the chimney are sitting in front of you. If you look up towards the ceiling... this is one of the middle poles [drawing a picture of a single pole with a sloping roof]. Did you see any rafters going this way [with bracing extending horizontally from the pole] or did they all go up to the top? From the side? Do you recall?

MS. PARKER: That way.

MR. AWAKUNI-SWETLAND: Like this? Okay, so there was nothing... It wasn't running...r

MS. PARKER: No. There was no other braces.

MR. AWAKUNI-SWETLAND: So there wasn't, nothing like this [pointing to the horizontal braces in the drawing]. They all went up like that [rafters converging at the peak of the pole].

MS. PARKER: I guess. I never noticed that. It must have been pretty sturdy too. Cured wood.

MR. AWAKUNI-SWETLAND: Okay. And that was remodeled?

MS. PARKER: Several times. But I don't remember who did it.

MR. AWAKUNI-SWETLAND: Okay.

MS. PARKER: Whether the people who belonged in this group here, or other members of the tribe that wanted to use it. I don't know. But it was always kept up and repaired. Until the later years. Because I went up there with that other fellow [another researcher], I told you his name. His first name was Campbell. That's when I saw it. I couldn't believe it. The trees grew up so fast.

MR. AWAKUNI-SWETLAND: What was the name? Was it always called Horse Head lodge?

MS. PARKER: Yes.

MR. AWAKUNI-SWETLAND: Was there ever a Horse Head group? Or was it just the lodge you referred to.

MS. PARKER: I don't think anybody of that group called themselves Horse Head.

MR. AWAKUNI-SWETLAND: I know that Grandma and Grandpa [Charles and Elizabeth Stabler] always taught me that you don't name people that are gone. You don't talk about people that have passed away. But I think it could be helpful if we could know the family names of people that were in different groups. So I was wondering if you could remember what family people belonged to the Big Crazies?

Or if you know any that belonged to the Little Crazies? Did they dance at Horse Head lodge or did they go to his [Gilbert Morris] place?

MS. PARKER: More or less they were mingled. They'd mingle. Some of them would be up here and some of them would be down there. But they all knew where they belonged. Who they joined.

I've been to both places so I'd see the same people over there as was at the Horse Head lodge.

MR. AWAKUNI-SWETLAND: Do you remember any difference between how the Horse Head lodge looked inside and how the Gilbert lodge looked inside?

MS. PARKER: Similar. There was no difference.

MR. AWAKUNI-SWETLAND: They had a chimney in it? And posts.

MS. PARKER: Uh-hum. Stove - everything to cook with. It didn't have stove lids like we've got on ours stoves or even those old fashioned stoves. It just had legs on it with a great big kettle sitting right in it. That's the way it was. They put their meat in there. That's the way it was.

MR. AWAKUNI-SWETLAND: So the kettle sat kind of down into that stove?

MS. PARKER: Yeah. Somebody sold that. I don't know who. That big iron kettle. My dad went up to get it one time to put it away or bring it here and put it away. No kettle. They left it there in case somebody else wanted to use it. But they never saved it.

MR. AWAKUNI-SWETLAND: What time would people usually gather for an activity?

MS. PARKER: Oh, all hours after lunch. After lunch. All hours they would come, Some of them would have to cook. Some would make fire, clean up. Then people, the majority of the ones would come, oh, anywhere from 5:30 or so. The doings most generally lasted up to 10:30 — 11:00 o'clock at night.

MR. AWAKUNI-SWETLAND: Of course now, when you were up there last time [to the Horse Head lodge site] with that other fellow, you saw it looked *uchizhe* again, just brushy.

MS. PARKER: Yeah.

MR. AWAKUNI-SWETLAND: Was it that way when people were using it?

MS. PARKER: No. It was always... it was blue grass. It was smooth. [Of] course people parked all over. You know that was horse and buggy days. There was very few cars. We were one of them that had cars. My grandpa Henry Turner, he had a car and John Turner. And there was some other people, I can't remember who. We had to have something like that to make that distance down here, to home.

Lodges east of Macy...

MR. AWAKUNI-SWETLAND: You mentioned the Silas Woods place east of Macy as one place that they had that *xube wachigaxe* [sacred dance]. Do you remember the lodge that was there?

MS. PARKER: There's no lodge there, just a house. They put up a tent.

My dad said that we're not suppose to know about those doings or make it our business.

MR. AWAKUNI-SWETLAND: Let me show you a picture and see what you think of it [looking at the Silas Wood dance lodge of the 1920s]

MS. PARKER: That must be before my day. I never saw that. That was before my days. The first time I ever went to one of them [powwows] was right there in Macy, where that Macy school is? That was a powwow ground then. That's the first time I ever went to powwow.

MR. WALKER: About 1922.

MR. AWAKUNI-SWETLAND: About 1922? Okay. I have a couple of enlarged pictures that may be easier to see. This [lodge] has planks for the side, big windows, and doorway. "Standing Hawk Lodge", *a* [it says]. *Gthedo^{n}no^{n}zhi^n* [Hawk Standing, a personal name]. I guess he had a lodge. But this is way back there [in time].

MS. PARKER: *Gthedo^{n}no^{n}zhi^n*, hmm...

Talking about the Warren Davis lodge...

MR. WALKER: [describing the Hiram Mitchell lodge] That was a peyote group. They're called Native American [Church] now. It was a peyote organization that had that lodge built. The fireplace — kind of half moon like. Built in concrete but now, these other fireplaces — they use a spade and dig it out on the ground. But this one was solid concrete.

That's what I told him [indicating Awakuni-Swetland] about it and we stopped over there at the place. He asked the folks [who are living there now] if he could go over there. He thinks that the concrete fireplace is still out there. That I don't know. They might have tore it up when they took that lodge and moved it over here to Pete Blackbird's place.

Then someway, *Wahoⁿthiⁿge* [Orphans], someway, somehow, I don't know, they moved that lodge again over here to Warren Davis'. Right back there in that valley.

MS. PARKER: Yeah. See I told you I didn't know who moved that.

MR. AWAKUNI-SWETLAND: But you've been there?

MS. PARKER: Yeah.

MR. AWAKUNI-SWETLAND: You remember seeing it there?

MS. PARKER: Yeah.

MR. AWAKUNI-SWETLAND: [looking at a topographic map] Here's the highway [75]. So you're coming west and there's that little road that goes off to that church farm. So you keep going here and there's that little valley. This is the valley in here. There is a well...

MS. PARKER: uh-hum, Used to be.

MR. AWAKUNI-SWETLAND: A little round stock tank, *egoⁿ* [like]. Where was the lodge from that?

MS. PARKER: [points to an area north of the gravel road in the valley].

AWAKUNI SWETLAND to MR. WALKER: About where you said?

MR. WALKER: Yeah.

MR. AWAKUNI-SWETLAND: Good! Do you remember hearing a name? If somebody said if they were going to the lodge, did they name it?

MS. PARKER: Old skunks. Old Skunks

MR. WALKER: Yeah.

MS. PARKER: That's the only one... And there was the Little Skunks too.

MR. AWAKUNI-SWETLAND: *Moⁿgazhiⁿga*

MS. PARKER: Uh-hum. I don't know whether they celebrated in the same building or what. Gee, there was a lot of people on this reservation. And there ain't none, now.

Lodges west of Macy...

MR. AWAKUNI-SWETLAND: What about west? We haven't gone west, yet, from Macy.

MS. PARKER: Just that Wind Lodge. I don't know whose land it sat on. I just know it was there. I don't think I ever went there either. Never. For any celebration.

MR. AWAKUNI-SWETLAND: Do you know any of the folks that were that way?

MS. PARKER: Hmm...I was thinking that old man Parrish Saunsoci, him and his old lady Clementine. I think they were one couple that went over there. And another man, whether they joined in there or not, they called him "Big", but I don't know why, John Lyons.

MS. PARKER to MR. WALKER: Was that Herman's dad? John Lyons? Or you don't remember?

MR. WALKER: Nicholas. They called him Jim.

MS. PARKER: Jim?

MR. WALKER: Yeah. In school days. School days they called him Jim.

MS. PARKER: I always... we always knew him by John.

MR. WALKER: But his real name was Nicholas.

END TAPE

Appendix E
JOE AND IRENE GILPIN
July 7, 1992

Joseph A. Gilpin was born in 1914 and resided with his family along the Missouri River north of Decatur, Nebraska. He courted and married Irene Harlan (born 1919) who lived closer to Macy. Like many fortunate Omaha children, Irene spent much of her young life in the company of her grandparents, Mr. and Mrs. Paul Thomas. Joe and Irene spent the majority of their married life in Omaha, Nebraska, working, raising a family, and finally retiring.

Through the extensive and complex kinship system of the Omaha people I had a distant knowledge of Joe and Irene, and used the terms "Grandmother" and "Grandfather" when visiting with them. In 1986, I was advised to seek assistance from Joe Gilpin in remedying a physiological ailment that had stymied treatment by western-trained medical personnel. The malady was recognized by discerning Omahas as *mu'sisi*, and Joe was acknowledged as a reputable doctor for this condition. I approached Joe and Irene in their home in a traditional Omaha manner of supplication, with gifts of food and tobacco. At the conclusion of the first treatment Irene provided a meal and Joe announced his desire to change the term of relationship that we had previously used. He was thankful for the manner in which I had approached him for help, attributed the correctness of my behavior to the elder relatives who had trained me, and declared that from now on, I was "his". In other words, he would call me "Son", and directed me to call his wife "Mother." Hence some of the references in the following transcriptions to these terms of relationship.

Joe and Irene were asked to assist in the dance lodge project due to their origins and early childhoods spent in regions of the Omaha Reservation in which lodge organizations were known to have been active. Both elders proved to be articulate in their description of lodges, families, and associated activities. In some instances their information and experiences complemented each other. In other instances, due to their disparate childhood

143

home neighborhood experiences, each could provide unique data. Joe and Irene were interviewed in their home at Omaha, Nebraska.

The Matthew Tyndall lodge...

MR. GILPIN: Because I know I ain't going to be too much of a help, but like I say, I was born and raised down there by the river. I didn't even know my own people. I went to [country day] school there. I thought I was the only Omaha there, you know. And I was never was around up there. But I do remember this one [dance lodge] that was close to that old man Paul [Thomas]. But at that time, and I seen that, it was used by cattle [as a] shed. Cattle came in from all angles. There was no door for it. It was just about had it... done for.

MR. AWAKUNI-SWETLAND: That's the one over by Paul's place?

MR. GILPIN: Yeah. I remember seeing that.

MR. AWAKUNI-SWETLAND: Now, maybe you can help me with directions. [While consulting a topographic map of Macy] Here's Blackbird Creek. Macy is right here. And this is that road that goes south. Here's Lawrence and Catherine [Gilpin's] place, so this is the road that goes out. And right here is that *Mazi* Tyndall's place, the farm. The farm buildings are here and the trees extend — it might have been a curve like this. Now, that road goes up that hill and just before it gets here into this corner, there's a section line. Now is that the Paul Thomas place on this side of the section line?

MR. GILPIN: Yeah, south side.

MR. AWAKUNI-SWETLAND: And *Mazi* Tyndall was on the north side?

MR. GILPIN: The north side.

MR. AWAKUNI-SWETLAND: Okay. And here's that line, that front line of the trees and this is all cornfield in here, now. Where do you remember that lodge sitting? There's a windmill back in them trees, about there.

MR. GILPIN: If I remember, I saw it right here. Right kind of southeast of the house, over — along in there is where I thought I remember. I was small, too.

MRS. GILPIN: I remember it — When I've seen it, this is the way I remember it. Now, right along the fence there, *Mazi*, coming down from my grandparents' place there's this line here.

MR. AWAKUNI-SWETLAND: Yes.

MRS. GILPIN: And right there is another line going up south.

MR. AWAKUNI-SWETLAND: Yes, okay.

MRS. GILPIN: And then down — You go down the hill here. There's a ditch right here. And up here stands a little kind of a shack where people lived. Right here, I don't know whose place that was. Anyway there was another windmill there in that little — around that shack. And right across from this little shack, there's a little, kind of a flat piece right here, like that. That's where I think I've seen that [lodge].

MR. GILPIN: That's where I saw it.

MRS. GILPIN: Right across from where Poker Bill (?) used to live.

MR. GILPIN: Where that hill is, where you come up the hill from Macy, it's down there just about where that flat is down there. Well, there's a little house there, a windmill. Well, it's right on that flat. That's about where I remember it.

MRS. GILPIN: See, where this house is, there's a road right along here.

MR. GILPIN: That goes over west.

MRS. GILPIN: And that windmill you're talking about is down here. And down in the ditch, you might say, then this lodge was right here, right across from this house.

MR. AWAKUNI-SWETLAND: Right across from that house. And your...

MRS. GILPIN: My grandparents lived up here.

MR. AWAKUNI-SWETLAND: ...grandparents were up there. Okay.

MR. GILPIN: Yeah, I remember seeing that. I don't know. Dad went out west, along in there, for something. And I was — as many kids as dad had it seemed like sometime I was the one to go along. They took me. And I remember. But it wasn't being used, it was getting pretty well [caved in] — when I saw it.

MR. AWAKUNI-SWETLAND: Can you give me a range of dates when you saw it and it was being used by cattle, about when was that? About how old were you?

MR. GILPIN: About, I would say, it might have been around '21, '22 — 1922. Because right along there dad sent us to school, out to Genoa and I was there in the fall of '23, I believe, or '24 I was out there. So, it must have been about 1921 or '22 that I remember seeing that. But nobody, no humans were using it then. It was kind of a more or less a shed then.

MRS. GILPIN: I don't know what society had that, or used that.

MR. AWAKUNI-SWETLAND: How would — If you wanted to describe, "I'm going over to this lodge over here," would you have had a name for it when it was sitting there? You know, like, if you were going to the Little Skunk Lodge, everybody knew where that was, or Horse Head Lodge. But when it was sitting here at that time, how would you describe, "I'm going over there." How would you say where you were going?

MR. GILPIN: God, I don't know that.

MRS. GILPIN: I'd just say we were going to the dance. It was where they were having the dance.

MR. AWAKUNI-SWETLAND: But the lodge itself, the building, didn't have a name at that time?

MRS. GILPIN: I was too small to remember. But I remember that.

MR. GILPIN: Yeah, I just remember — I'm just like her, I remember seeing it. And I didn't live by it. I was totally a stranger up there.

MR. AWAKUNI-SWETLAND: Yeah, you lived further south [a few miles].

MR. GILPIN: Yeah, clear over by the Missouri River.

MR. AWAKUNI-SWETLAND: What were you doing sneaking around up north like that?

MR. GILPIN: I was sneaking on her.

MRS. GILPIN: I wasn't probably even around.

MR. GILPIN: I think we went over the hill out west, dad did. I don't remember. It must have been a feast or something and when we come back I saw it again, when we came back. It was up, but cattle were coming in and out.

MRS. GILPIN: At the time I remembered it, it was still owned by the Indians, theTyndall's. I've seen them at that big house. So, I don't remember cattles going in that lodge. It was vacant, though. Nobody was using it anymore.

MR. AWAKUNI-SWETLAND: Any idea when it finally fell down or was removed?

MR. GILPIN: That I don't know.

MRS. GILPIN: I don't remember that either.

Lodges further south...

MR. AWAKUNI-SWETLAND: I've heard stories that there was another house that started at Hiram Mitchell's place, along Woods Creek just north of Decatur, just west-northwest of Decatur, there. That it started there and then later it got took over by another group. They moved it, I think, Bert Fremont and them guys were involved. They moved it up to Pete Blackbird's place. And then from there it got moved again and went down to by Warren Davis's place. Now which house was that?

MRS. GILPIN: Old Skunks.

MR. AWAKUNI-SWETLAND: That's the Old Skunks.

MR. GILPIN: Old Skunks. There was the Young Skunks.

MRS. GILPIN: They called them *Mo^{n}gai^{n}sh?age* [Old Skunk].

MR. GILPIN: And *Mo^{n}gazhi^{n}ga* [Litle or Young Skunks]. Because they didn't have nothing. They were just like me.

MR. AWAKUNI-SWETLAND: They didn't have a lodge?

MR. GILPIN: No.

MRS. GILPIN: They just had their hand games in private places like private homes. But they had a real pleasant time.

MR. AWAKUNI-SWETLAND: Who belonged to the Old Skunks? I know that it's inappropriate to name people's names who are gone, but I hope you can overlook that because here's where we can find out, you know, who belonged to what.

MR. GILPIN: Well, I'll tell you. Dad was in it, but he couldn't maintain himself to be of any service to the group at all, because he was farming. He had 13 of us. He had to up and get to getting, for our survival, farming. He couldn't put his time over there. Just once in a while he would, you know, see them and let them know that he was still with them. But I do remember Old Man Joe Dick. Old Man Charlie Grant and there was Morgan Grant and there was Old Man William Sherman and there was others there, too, I believe, but I can't — I don't know their names. But I do remember them. Yeah, they all must have been carpenters because they built it. They all got together.

MR. AWAKUNI-SWETLAND: They built the lodge?

MR. GILPIN: They built the lodge. Them guys, yeah. All Indians, no White men in there.

MR. AWAKUNI-SWETLAND: Where did they build it at?

MR. GILPIN: Right southwest corner there's 80 acres that belonged to Warren Davis. That southwest corner, just at the very corner where that hill comes in, it was just right in there, that flat place. And there's one cottonwood tree that's towards that corner, right in there they had that. Oh, I imagine it's about over 50 feet by 150 feet away from the south edge of that line, going east away from there. That's at the south edge of that.

It was a big one. That was real huge. And the structure of it, you know, them Indians were pretty smart. They built that, to have it clearly, they just had that one pole in the middle. Everything was tied from the center to the outside wall of that. It was all kind of partitioned, see. All the way around. The rafters all tied down, but I imagine that that's something I never paid no attention to. Was they had to be doubled to each one in order to hold up the roof. And it was all shingled, no tar paper, then. You know, it was all shingled. They really made a good lodge there.

MR. AWAKUNI-SWETLAND: Do you remember if they had — you know how a lot of those roofs — the roof line comes up and they have that little short, kind of like building with a little roof on it?

MR. GILPIN: Like an Eskimo igloo that sticks out?

MR. AWAKUNI-SWETLAND: Yeah.

MR. GILPIN: This one didn't have it. They were just complete round — oval — round, no piece tied to it. But inside they built, along the walls of it, why they cooked outside and when it was done they brought it in and put it on the tables along the edge of the wall. But just on one side.

MR. AWAKUNI-SWETLAND: Which side?

MR. GILPIN: The north side.

MR. AWAKUNI-SWETLAND: It would be on the north side of it. How did you get heat in there?

MR. GILPIN: I don't think they used it in the wintertime. This was too big. I've seen one that I went to once. That was up to — it's not too long ago, either, that one. We was down here [living in Omaha]. We went up there. They had a great big stove, made out of — I don't even think it was a regular stove. They made it — I mean, they had a pile of wood. And it rained just before we were going to go. It rained and snowed and it froze. Boy, we had a terrible time getting out of Omaha. We just barely made that last hill, at the Red Apple Farm [north of Omaha], west of that road, just barely made it. I remember it, it was wintertime. And I mean, they poured the wood to that thing, but boy I was sitting in the back all cuddled up away from it. It was too far away. But anyway, it was too cold. That was the first and the only time I've been in the lodge. The first time for the winter, that is.

MR. AWAKUNI-SWETLAND: For the wintertime.

Which lodge? That was one of those —

MR. GILPIN: That was down there where Ted Morris and them lived, down in there, Henry Turner. There was a lodge down there. I don't know what they called that.

MR. AWAKUNI-SWETLAND: Yeah, along Horse Head Creek?

MR. GILPIN: Yeah, I guess it was.

MR. AWAKUNI-SWETLAND: Was it the Horse Head Lodge?

MR. GILPIN: Yeah.

MR. AWAKUNI-SWETLAND: Did you hear about the lodge that was at Gilbert Morris's place, just north?

MR. GILPIN: I was there just once, that's all. I never had gotten to know anything about that either. So, I couldn't tell you nothing about neither of them, the Horse Head and that one. I don't even know the name of that one myself.

MR. AWAKUNI-SWETLAND: Well, let's go back to the Old Skunks, since you're more familiar with the folks down south. Do you remember hearing anything about the Old Skunk Lodge before it went to the Warren Davis place?

MR. GILPIN: Nope, that I don't really know and I've never heard, either. And, in fact, I didn't even know that they had another one. That's the only one that I know of.

MR. AWAKUNI-SWETLAND: The only one.

MR. GILPIN: Yeah. I was in Genoa then and I heard — we come home for vacation and they said they were building it. And they were all, see they were donating and having dinner together, too, you know. They go there, early and they were making it. I didn't see them — I didn't get to see none of them working at it, either, I just heard that because dad was in it. But dad was always too busy. He didn't have that time to help them build it, either.

MR. AWAKUNI-SWETLAND: So, that would have been the early '20s, because you were already at Genoa in '23?

MR. GILPIN: Yeah.

MR. AWAKUNI-SWETLAND: What happened to that lodge? It's not there now.

MR. GILPIN: Yeah. I don't remember when they tore it up. It seemed like the later years, the time, the times were changing to where people had to —there wasn't nothing up there to make any living, unless you worked for a farmer. Everything was just to the point where it was pressing. So, it seemed like everybody, you know, couldn't stay with the good times. Everybody was way apart and it seemed like — but what year it was that they tore it down, I don't remember. That I couldn't tell you.

MR. AWAKUNI-SWETLAND: Would it have been before World War II, after World War II, roughly?

MR. GILPIN: It must have been up in —

MRS. GILPIN: After the war.

MR. GILPIN: — in the '20s I believe that was tore down.

MR. AWAKUNI-SWETLAND: Well, they built it in the '20s.

MR. GILPIN: Yeah. And it could have been still in the '20s. Or maybe it was still there. Because when I come home in '29, I didn't go no wheres. I worked on the farms. I didn't even go to town. I bring my money home and give it to dad to "buy something to eat, dad." And I stayed home and when everybody was gone at dusk, I just go down to the water tank and take a good bath and had a good rest. So, I didn't put my time nowheres else, you know, in order to survive.

MRS. GILPIN: You mean that lodge, are you still talking about the lodge?

MR. AWAKUNI-SWETLAND: Yeah, the Old Skunk.

MRS. GILPIN: Old Skunk.

MR. AWAKUNI-SWETLAND: Yeah, the *Mo^{n}gai^{n}sh?age*. He remembers hearing about it being built when he came back from Genoa in the early '20s and they were building it then. But we're trying to figure out what happened to it. Where did it go? When did it quit existing?

MR. GILPIN: I went by there that one year, but it wasn't used. Just mostly everybody kind of faded out, like, but it was there. A lot of weeds around it.

MRS. GILPIN: I've got another one that's good for you to talk to. Minnie Blackbird. That was on her dad's land. She's still going around with her daughter, Grace. Grace takes care of her, now. That was her dad's land where they had that Skunk Lodge — the Old Skunk Lodge.

MR. AWAKUNI-SWETLAND: Warren Davis?

MRS. GILPIN: Uh-huh. Yeah, she would be a good one to talk to.

Describing a Pipe Dance...

MRS. GILPIN: I went to some of those doings since I was a little girl because of my grandparents — I stayed with my grandparents a lot and they'd go to those things and they'd take me to them. Then, there was another deal they called *Wawao^n*. Have you ever heard of that, *Wawao^n*?

MR. AWAKUNI-SWETLAND: That's where they have two staffs of feathers [hanging] down like this?

MRS. GILPIN: I've seen that just one time. I guess my dad, *ishtiawo^n*. Because my grandma had a little bundle like that. She had Indian paint and plume put away, but it was used for my dad at the time. But, you know, they never thought much about it, I guess, like these folks do [referring to the Gilpin side]. They think a lot of that, because his brother Isaac [Gilpin], *ishtego^{n}ite awo^n*. But my dad and my grandma, they never spoke of it. I just heard grandma talk about it when we went to see that one that they had. I remember it was for Willis Woodhull's mother, Eva Kemp. Towards morning I remember grandma woke us up, me and my brother. We were right there all night at this. She woke us up so we could see that towards morning, I believe it was. That some old man brought her in on his back. He had a blanket over her. And she was all painted up. I remember that. And that's the only one that I ever seen.

MR. AWAKUNI-SWETLAND: How old were you?

MRS. GILPIN: A year-and-a-half.

MR. AWAKUNI-SWETLAND: Yeah, yeah, yeah. Dad robbed the cradle on you.

MRS. GILPIN: I must have been, say — I remember it, so I must have been like six — in the '20s.

MR. AWAKUNI-SWETLAND: Where did they have that dance at?

MRS. GILPIN: That I always thought, but I know at that time that Little Crazy's Lodge wasn't there. It was in a lodge.

MR. AWAKUNI-SWETLAND: It was in a lodge?

MRS. GILPIN: Uh-huh. It might have been the Big Crazies lodge or maybe the one towards south, I don't know. It's been a long — Maybe it was that Big Skunk — I mean Old Skunks Lodge. That I don't remember. But I remember that night that we were there and that was going on.

Lodges and Groups North of Macy...

MR. AWAKUNI-SWETLAND: You mentioned the Little Crazy's. Where was their lodge at?

MRS. GILPIN: Gilbert Morris's land.

MR. AWAKUNI-SWETLAND: That was Gilbert Morris's land.

MRS. GILPIN: Right north of Macy, there.

MR. AWAKUNI-SWETLAND: Do you remember who some of those folks were that went over to Little Crazy's?

MRS. GILPIN: Yeah, Ted Morris, Gilbert Morris, Henry Turner. There were a lot of them but I can't remember. Ted White. And probably Dan Walker. Sam Parker. John McCauley, too, I think.

MR. AWAKUNI-SWETLAND: John McCauley?

MRS. GILPIN: And Ben Parker, I think.

MR. AWAKUNI-SWETLAND: Ben Parker?

MRS. GILPIN: Uh-huh. Because I used to see them around there.

MR. AWAKUNI-SWETLAND: They were the Little Crazy's? $Gtho^nthi^nzhi^nga$.

MRS. GILPIN: Uh-huh.

MR. AWAKUNI-SWETLAND: The Big Crazies, they were a group but they danced at the Horse Head Lodge, is that right? So, the Horse Head Lodge is the name of the building.

MR. GILPIN: Horse Head Lodge, right.

MR. AWAKUNI-SWETLAND: But the group was the Big Crazies? $Gtho^nthi^nto^nga$

MRS. GILPIN: Uh-huh. Yeah.

MR. GILPIN: Yeah.

MRS. GILPIN: Maybe those was most of the same bunch there, I don't know.

MR. AWAKUNI-SWETLAND: What about the *Hethushka zhi^nga* [Little Warriors]? Where did they come in?

MRS. GILPIN: My son, Charlie Stabler was one. My dad was one. That's all I know. And to my thinking, this Old Lady Solomon — Harry Solomon's wife had a — she must have had an older son, a Saunsoci, and he was one of them. I think — he died.

MR. AWAKUNI-SWETLAND: That's Minnie?

MRS. GILPIN: Minnie Solomon. I guess that was her name, that Old Lady Solomon. Howard's grandma.

MR. AWAKUNI-SWETLAND: Yeah, I believe so.

MRS. GILPIN: And that's all I remember.

Other Groups...

MR. AWAKUNI-SWETLAND: *Waho^nthi^nge* [Orphans], have you ever heard of them up at Macy?

MRS. GILPIN: Uh-huh, yeah. And that was like Bert Fremont and them, *Waho^nthi^nge*. Bert Fremont, Paul Fremont, I guess. And Dave Canby. And Neil Mitchell, I think. Wasn't that *Paho^ngamo^nthi^n*'s dad?

MR. GILPIN: *Paho^ngamo^nthi^n*'s dad, yeah.

MRS. GILPIN: He was Bert Fremont's brother-in-law, I think, Neil Mitchell.

MR. GILPIN: Yeah.

MRS. GILPIN: * * *.

MR. GILPIN: What was his name?

MRS. GILPIN: Who?

MR. GILPIN: Roy Mitchell's dad, Neil. Neil Mitchell.

MRS. GILPIN: Gee, I don't know. I don't remember.

MR. GILPIN: I used to know.

MRS. GILPIN: I know Roy Hips, one of his boys, they had that name and he's got that name, Neil, too.

MR. GILPIN: Yeah, I can't think of that name.

MR. AWAKUNI-SWETLAND: Mitchells, aren't they I^n*kesabe* [Black Shoulder Buffalo Clan]?

MRS. GILPIN: Uh-huh, yeah. Well, that *Paho^{n}gamo^{n}thi^n*, he's still living at that health center. And Roy Mitchell, he's still living too.

MR. AWAKUNI-SWETLAND: I heard just this week about a group that called themselves the Opossums.

MRS. GILPIN: Maybe that was you guys [teasing her husband].

MR. GILPIN: Maybe that was me. Opossum, *I^{n}shti^{n}pe*.

MR. AWAKUNI-SWETLAND: Well, let's see... what name... *Ixasto^n*.

MRS. GILPIN: Yeah, I heard of them.

MR. GILPIN: I didn't know them.

MRS. GILPIN: *Ixasto^n* were way down south.

MR. GILPIN: That would be west from where we are, yeah west, I guess.

MRS. GILPIN: I've heard of them but I don't know who they could be.

MR. GILPIN: [switching to another group] There was a few of them that I do remember. *Mo^{n}zeska no^{n}p?i^n* [Money Necklace]. Annie Guitar, Charlie Guitar.

MRS. GILPIN: Isaac Sherman.

MR. GILPIN: Isaac Sherman. Them guys were the cheese, Isaac Sherman and them.

MRS. GILPIN: Big wheels.

MR. GILPIN: And *Paho^{n}gamo^{n}thi^n* and them, they were in there.

MR. AWAKUNI-SWETLAND: What did their name translate out to?

MR. GILPIN: money necklace.

MR. GILPIN: *** .

MR. AWAKUNI-SWETLAND: Okay, yeah.

MRS. GILPIN: Yeah, it's a great big thing, nickel or whatever. It's a great big thing.

MR. AWAKUNI-SWETLAND: That peace medal with that man's face on it and all of that?

MRS. GILPIN: Uh-huh.

MR. GILPIN: They brought that back from Washington.

MR. AWAKUNI-SWETLAND: Yeah, those are peace medals.

MR. GILPIN: That's where Uncle Sam got his finger right in there to the tribal ways, trying them to make them live the way he want's them to live. When this guy was going, don't let them put that on you. You know, when he come back, he had that on. He was a big shot.

MRS. GILPIN: It had something to do with the patent fee, didn't it?

MR. GILPIN: Yeah. If he hadn't of [put that peace medal on], we would have had our reservation full... today. But this guy here signed it and they put that *mo^{n}zeska wano^{n}p?i^n* on him. Big man. They didn't want him, but this guy signed it. So everybody took over the old land and what they had they sold it and they kept selling it and selling it, you know.

MR. AWAKUNI-SWETLAND: I heard of another group, even another group — boy, I'm hearing of more groups up there, called the — Emily [Parker] didn't know what to call it in Omaha, but she said their name was White Riders. The White Riders group.

MRS. GILPIN: *Ska agthi^n*. I heard of them.

MR. AWAKUNI-SWETLAND: *Ska agthi^n*. That would make sense, yeah. White Riders.

MRS. GILPIN: That was like my grandpa, Ralph Dixon and White Webster. But I don't know all the members either, but I know they were in there.

MR. GILPIN: [laughing] Now I know I never knew nothing, down by the river, that's all I know. The Missouri River. I never did hear of them.

MR. AWAKUNI-SWETLAND: What kind of a group was it?

MRS. GILPIN: Well, I guess they just go by their — wherever they lived, their neighbors or something, I think, that's the way it was. They were about the same age and maybe relatives. That's what I think. Because if there's a bunch they were mostly relatives.

MR. AWAKUNI-SWETLAND: What kind of activities would they have?

MRS. GILPIN: Same thing, hand games.

MR. AWAKUNI-SWETLAND: Hand games.

MRS. GILPIN: That was like where that Fish Walker, around that area, I think.

MR. GILPIN: [switching to another group]I was down there when they started that group. I was in on it, too — I was in it, I remember. *Wai azhi.*

MR. AWAKUNI-SWETLAND: *Wai azhi?* What does that mean?

MR. GILPIN: You don't say much.

MRS. GILPIN: Quiet. Like if I don't talk much, that's what they used to say about me, because I would never say much when I was young, I mean little.

MR. GILPIN: A quiet person.

MRS. GILPIN: That's what my Grandpa Thomas used to say about me [laughs].

MR. AWAKUNI-SWETLAND: What kind of a group did you have?

MR. GILPIN: Just like the other groups, just people. All the Grants, two Grants, Old Morgan and Charlie and the rest of us were young ones, and Charlie's boys and Morgan's boys. He had only one boy. And them. And there was some Morris' from Macy that would come down there and they'd included themselves in *Wai azhi.*

MRS. GILPIN: Them *Mo^{n}gazhi^{n}ga*'s, they were mostly neighbors, enit?

MR. GILPIN: Yeah.

MRS. GILPIN: Like Cabney Pappan, Grandpa Clyde [Hallowell?].

Shinny Ball Game...

MR. GILPIN: Oh, yeah. In the vicinity of the place they start up a group there. And over here they'd start up a group. Well, it was the only thing we went to. No ball games, no shows.

MRS. GILPIN: Shinny games.

MR. GILPIN: Well, shinny games, boy that was a lot of fun. Man, that's a rough game, too. That's just like hockey, only it's a ball on the ground, no ice. Boy, man, I mean, that's kind of rough, too. But there's rules and regulations and my clan, *Ko^{n}ze*, they are the ones. They're the directors that tell you, they talk to you. You've got to play and [they[give out the rules. How to hit the ball and don't use *a ga a.* If you're going to go and hit that ball, don't use your stick up over... That might take his club away and hurt somebody. Or hit him in the face and knock his eye out or something. But my clan used to take over and tell them the rules and regulations.

Boy, that's a good — I used to — Boy, Sundays they'd play. You'd be up there by noon, I'd be there. They had a hay meadow there. When they get that cutting off, then we'd go in there and play. Two stakes, just like hockey, only hockey has got a little hoop in it.

MR. AWAKUNI-SWETLAND: Oh, the goal post.

MR. GILPIN: We had two goals just like a football [game]. You'd kick it in between the goals. You'd have two stakes up and you'd run your ball through and you got a point.

MR. AWAKUNI-SWETLAND: How far apart were those posts?

MR. GILPIN: Well, they could be quite a distance, too. If there were a lot of them [playing].

MR. AWAKUNI-SWETLAND: Oh, your field length.

MR. GILPIN: Yeah, field length. About like a football field. About that distance, too. A long ways apart Yeah, that's a lot of fun, shinny game.

MR. AWAKUNI-SWETLAND: And your goal posts, your two sticks, how far apart would they be, just one-man wide?

MR. GILPIN: No, they were about six-feet.

MR. AWAKUNI-SWETLAND: Outstretched arms. How many people played on a team?

MR. GILPIN: Well, it varies, whoever all was there with a stick. You throw it in a pile and mix them up and then blindfold a guy with a handkerchief for him, and then he sits down and throws one stick over here and one stick over there and that's the teams and they play against one another. Yeah, boy, that was a lot of fun.

MR. AWAKUNI-SWETLAND: So, it wouldn't be like the *Hethushka zhi^{n}ga* come down and they want to play the *Mo^{n}gazhi^{n}ga*, it's not going to be that way, they are going to mix themselves all up and make new teams.

MR. GILPIN: Yeah. Form a new team every time they play. It ain't a certain bunch over here. No. Whoever it comes in, then they split the pile up and make up a team. And then there's a stake... maybe a horse, maybe a blanket, and the winner takes it. Or there's money and so they play hard for that. Sometimes there's a hog. You're going to eat. They play hard.

MR. AWAKUNI-SWETLAND: What score would you play for?

MR. GILPIN: Well, that's — They don't play for a score, it's whatever can be made, maybe three, four, whatever they make. The more points you make is the winner. It's just like hockey, the same thing. It plays the same way but hockey they are on the ice. Same thing.

MR. AWAKUNI-SWETLAND: Grandpa Charlie [Stabler] used to tell me about, he used to make them shinny sticks. He described them as ash or hickory, about that big around [indicating about 1-1/2 to 2 inch diameter]?

MR. GILPIN: Hickory is the best.

MR. AWAKUNI-SWETLAND: Like a cane turned upside down, he said.

MR. GILPIN: We'd take a good-sized young hickory growing off of a stump. They stool out, kinda' long, they are the best. A regular tree, no. But more or less from a tree that's been cut, it stools and they're long. That's where you get your... [stick]. Hickory is the best. It isn't heavy. It's hard wood, but it ain't too hard, and you take it and bend it over. Tie it with wire, bent. You could heat it over a fire and cook the juice out of it and then it's going to stay that way. Leave it cold, leave it lay for a day or so. When you take that wire off that hook is there. Trim it up. Fix up the handle good. Then you've got a shinny stick.

MR. AWAKUNI-SWETLAND: There's been a lot of people asking me stions about shinny in the last few years... if I've heard about it, if I've asked questions about it. What would it take to play a shinny game today? Do you think it would be possible for Omaha people to get together and play a shinny game today?

MR. GILPIN: Well, yes, it would, but they ain't got no grounds. There used to be — Now, they've got a damn swimming pool where they used to play [south of the Tribal Council Building in Macy]. That kind of makes for tight quarters. There's enough ground there. They used to use that whole place there, in Macy there. Boy, Man, there used to be a lot of them. They'd all go out there.

MRS. GILPIN: Anybody could play that. You don't have to be a member to that or anything like that.

MR. GILPIN: As long as you've got a club, throw it in there and where ever side you're on you played on that side. There were many fights. Sometimes those guys that drink and then they'd get in there and play. They'd get in a fight and squabble and they'd pull them apart and go on with the shinny game. Just like hockey, you know. If there was a hot-tempered man in there, it would just get out-of-hand but they'd cool him down, penalize him and let him to sit down and cool off a bit.

MR. AWAKUNI-SWETLAND: Did women ever play in there?

MR. GILPIN: A game? They played — I don't know what they called it. I seen them playing.

MRS. GILPIN: They had a game of their own.

MR. GILPIN: It's a wheel. But they had — I think they had a stick with it, kind of similar to a shinny stick. It was a limb with a...

MRS. GILPIN: A cross-piece.

MR. GILPIN: Yeah, a cross-piece of it. They tried to roll that wheel up so that the wheel would roll. Push it, I mean, them young women can really play. And rough. They had them real long squaw dresses on. The last time I seen that was when they first moved over across the ditch where the pow-wow ground is now, down on the south end, there. It don't take a big place for women to — just for a few women to play. That's the first and last time I saw it. I heard about it. That one year I come home from school, I saw it played there. It was a lot of fun. They play hard, too. But theirs is not a ball, it's a wheel. The object is to roll that and take it away from them and try to get it to rolling. I don't know what they called that.

MRS. GILPIN: I don't either.

MR. GILPIN: Really I never did hear a name for it. I imagine they had a name for it.

The Moccasin Game...

MRS. GILPIN: They used to have on both sides, the men and the women. Instead of playing hand games they'd have, like, was it four moccasins, or two?

MR. GILPIN: Yeah, I saw that just once, too.

MRS. GILPIN: Was it four?

MR. GILPIN: Four.

MRS. GILPIN: Yeah. They'd hide that stone or the rock in one of those moccasins.

MR. GILPIN: The two.

MRS. GILPIN: And then they'd have —

MR. GILPIN: Four little bundles. They called it $hi^n beugtho^n$. It's like a sole. They would take it and roll it up and they'd put that stone in it, hi^n-$beugtho^n$. So, they'd kind of hide it, you know. You don't know which one has got it. Just like the two people getting up [in a hand game] with the four hands. But they had them four little bundle, *hi^{n}beugtho^n*.

MRS. GILPIN: I seen them play that — the Woods, like you're talking about, the Woods' place down there near Macy, that's where I seen them play that.

MR. GILPIN: Maybe Momma was there when I was there?

MRS. GILPIN: Maybe I was... [laughing].

MR. GILPIN: Yeah. I went there. And Henry Turner, the Old Man, the *u wasabe i.*

MRS. GILPIN: They had that, what do you call it, awning — a real long awning with that.

MR. GILPIN: I was there just once and seen that, one time.

MRS. GILPIN: It was made out of twigs and canvas, or tarp.

MR. AWAKUNI-SWETLAND: Kind of like an arbor?

MRS. GILPIN: Yeah, that's what it was, an arbor.

Lodges and Groups West of Macy...

MR. AWAKUNI-SWETLAND: Well, let's see, we've looked north, south and east. How about west. Wind Lodge. Have you ever heard of it?

MR. GILPIN: I've heard of it, that's all.

MRS. GILPIN: That was — That stood right across from the Jim McCauley's place.

MR. GILPIN: Oh, yeah. I never seen it but — I know it's gone but I heard them talk about it. There used to be a lodge there. Now they had a well down there. That's where they get their water, down in that, from the house, south there. Yeah, the lodge is gone.

MRS. GILPIN: I don't remember whose land that was. Maybe it was Jim McCauley's.

MR. GILPIN: Old man Sheridan lived there.

MRS. GILPIN: Yeah, but it wouldn't be his.

MR. GILPIN: Then I wouldn't know that.

MRS. GILPIN: Because them people, they didn't go to those things.

MR. AWAKUNI-SWETLAND: How about Harry Lyons, have you ever heard of him?

MRS. GILPIN: Yeah.

MR. AWAKUNI-SWETLAND: Wasn't his land right there.

MRS. GILPIN: uh-huh. That's where those Lyons' girls lived. Jim McCauley was with their mother. So, it must have been a Lyons' land.

MR. GILPIN: Yeah, it must have been.

MR. AWAKUNI-SWETLAND: [consulting a topographic map] When you go — If this is Macy here, and you got west, this is Blackbird Creek, so *Mazi* Tyndall's place is over here, the powwow grounds is over here, the projects. You go across that creek and come to that first four corners. Nowadays most everybody turns north. They turn north or south. But if you continued straight on west and go up that hill and down, there's a little creek down in here. Right in here was that lodge, Wind Lodge. Harry Lyons' place was over here on this side — the north side of the road. Right in here, on this side of the creek, just on the west side of that creek was a little one-room shack, [belonging to] Julia White Sheridan — Julia Sheridan White?

MRS. GILPIN: Her husband was Henry Sheridan.

MR. AWAKUNI-SWETLAND: Henry Sheridan. Okay. So, Julia White Sheridan. Continue on up to the next four corners — this is one mile from this road to this road. Here I've been told they had a powwow grounds.

MR. GILPIN: Powwow grounds, yeah. Dad used to go up and dance clear from down by the Missouri River [near Decatur], go on horseback. Clear up there to dance and get home a day later.

MRS. GILPIN: They built — They had bonfires up there.

MR. GILPIN: No electric lights.

MRS. GILPIN: No lights.

MR. GILPIN: Indians, a long time ago, were active. Get together and they would haul a lot of wood up there and dance by the light of that fire. They'd cook by it, they'd cook and they'd just have a hell of a time.

MR. AWAKUNI-SWETLAND: Your dad would come all of the way up to dance at this place?

MR. GILPIN: Way out there.

MRS. GILPIN: Way out west.

MR. AWAKUNI-SWETLAND: He had a white horse. He would always tell me he had a white horse. His dad bought him, grandpa bought him. Saddle him up, and put all his regalia around it and then he'd take off. Daylight he'd get home. He said that's quite a thing. You probably get the feeling. You like to dance. You get that blood into you, get working into yourself. He said no matter how far it is, you're going to go. Always go.
Yeah, up there on that flat is where they had their powwows, or any time there was any big doin's they'd have it up there. It's kind of flat, a big hill. It's flat up there, yeah. That's where — It's breezy.

MR. AWAKUNI-SWETLAND: And yet, you've got, down here on this creek, you've got timber, you've got water.

Did you ever heard about Lee Cayou and his merry-go-round? Is that true?

MRS. GILPIN: That was his grandpa. That wasn't Lee, was it?

MR. GILPIN: That was Old Man, that's my grandpa.

MR. AWAKUNI-SWETLAND: Your grandpa?

MR. GILPIN: Yeah, that's where I'd get my quarter blood, French.

MRS. GILPIN: His name wasn't Lee, was it? What was his name?

MR. GILPIN: Fred. Fred Cayou. The Old Man's Fred. Lee, that's one of his boys. That's my uncle.

MRS. GILPIN: He was married to Bertha Webster.

MR. GILPIN: Lee was. The old man Cayou, he was a white man, full blood

Frenchman. He come on over in a banana boat. He kinda come across and he didn't go back. But he worked himself this way until he got here and he got among the Indians and he liked it.

MRS. GILPIN: My mom said — she was a little girl at that time and she said they used to steal rides on his merry-go-round. No, I guess he'd really cuss them up.

MR. GILPIN: He was quite a cusser, I guess. He was a white man, you know. That language is his. Grandma used to tell, "Tell that White man go over the hill, somewheres, and let him use his language over there." You know — You probably know, we don't have cuss words like that.

MR. AWAKUNI-SWETLAND: Unh-unh, we don't.

MR. GILPIN: It's just like — *i^{n}desabe* [black face], *ishti^{n}thi^{n}ke* [monkey], or something like that.

MR. AWAKUNI-SWETLAND: Did you ever hear of the *Si sabe?* Black Feet?

MRS. GILPIN: Oh, yeah.

MR. GILPIN: *Si sabe?*

MR. AWAKUNI-SWETLAND: Oh, that's right. I shouldn't even be asking you. You go back to the Missouri River. Mom knows all about it [laughing].

MR. GILPIN: She should. She's lived right in Macy [laughing]

MRS. GILPIN: That was like my grandpa, Albert Robinson. I suppose my uncle John Robinson. I don't know that. Whoever belonged in that group, but I remember one of them was my grandpa, Albert Robinson. That's all I remember.

MR. AWAKUNI-SWETLAND: They were out west, also, right?

MRS. GILPIN: Uh-huh, right.

MR. AWAKUNI-SWETLAND: Because you had Robinsons over here.

MRS. GILPIN: Uh-huh. And I suppose Sam Black, he lived out there. But they go according to the age groups.

The Short Skirt Group...

MR. GILPIN: Let's see. Momma started a group. Right in Walthill.

MRS. GILPIN: I didn't start it, but we used to just play hand games, like — But we used to do that in Macy, too. But we didn't start anything. Just little girls. While we stayed there just over the winter. My uncle was in the hospital right there in Walthill. My dad had one brother and that was him. He took sick. He had cancer in his backbone, I guess. So, the family stayed up there in a little house at first, Ruth and Art Grant. Their grandma was my grandpa's cousin, I suppose. Her name was Irene Harlan Grant, that was her name. Because that's my name, now. We stayed there with them. Not with them, but Ruth and Art's little shack, we lived there. And we'd all, like Ida Parker, Ruth and Rachel Sheridan, but they were much older than we were. We'd all play hand games in grandma's middle room. She had a kitchen here and a front room over there. And we'd all play that. My uncle, Jack Thomas, he'd take care of the sticks.

MR. AWAKUNI-SWETLAND: Who would sing for you guys?

MRS. GILPIN: I don't remember. But my mom said that was Slim Parker, would sing for us. And then, yeah, pretty soon it got to be a regular group, you know. Older women joined in, like Addie and Dorothy Warner and —

MR. GILPIN: The wheel kept getting bigger and bigger.

MRS. GILPIN: And then there was an old lady, they called her Emma Ute. She was one of the types that liked to dress, you know, dressy, with make-up on and she'd wear her dresses real short, I guess, her squaw dresses real short. So they gave us the name of *Wachexe*.

MR. GILPIN: Short dresses.

MR. AWAKUNI-SWETLAND: Short dresses. *Wachexe*.

MRS. GILPIN: Uh-huh. And then it got to be bigger and bigger, so we didn't have no show.

MR. GILPIN: Crowded the little ones out, the big took over.

MR. AWAKUNI-SWETLAND: But that was just that short length of time in Walthill.

MRS. GILPIN: But I don't know if they went on after we moved home. When my uncle died, well we moved home and I never got to see them anymore. Because I was small. That's all we did was play hand games, like we've seen them play. That's what we used to do.

MR. GILPIN: As I say, it was just kids, young kids starting up. And then it got to be a big thing. A big group.

MRS. GILPIN: We would just bring cookies and grandma would make coffee for us. We'd all sit in and pretty soon — eating cookies and drinking coffee with them and spend our evenings that way.

Talking about the claims of who started the powwow...

MR. GILPIN: Them lodges, them Sioux built them. I guess that's about the way everybody built them. But as far as dancing, each tribe, they had their ways. There was nothing like what the Omaha had. But the Omaha's gave it to them for their amusement. But they had — each tribe — they all — some of them still use them, like Fire Dance [of the Apache], [for] that tribe, that's sacred. But they bring it up here. Performed that, and combined it with the Omaha powwow. They built that fire. And danced around it. They danced until that fire goes out.

MRS. GILPIN: Navajo's, wasn't it? Or Apache?

MR. AWAKUNI-SWETLAND: Apaches. Yeah.

MR. GILPIN: Yeah. But the Omaha's formed that by — They had their own, too, *washishka* [Shell Society, a sacred dance]. But this here, the war dance, they made that up. It's what everybody goes by now. What everybody has. I went and asked Old Man Turner. I heard the Winnebago say. I heard dad, Grandpa Hiram Mitchell, talk about it. Old times. Talk about how things went, and I heard them say that was created by the Omahas. This powwow, what they go by now. They had it and there were Indians scouting, maneuvering around. Heard a drum. They heard a drum and went to the sound of that drum. Here is was the Omahas, dancing. It was something different, to them And they liked it. It was theirs, They created it. And how it come about to be way, thanksgiving, giving thanks to Him [God]. And to celebrate.

I'm going to tell you kind of a sad story... but which has two different feelings. The time when they went to hunt, it was successful at times. And there was times, by God, it just's like a ball player. Getting up and trying to hit, gotta hit, and he can't. Ball's coming to him and he still can't hit it. They were out there hunting. It was mean and hard out there, where the animals were around. But they just couldn't contact them. It got to a point where they didn't have nothing. Nothing to eat. All they had was their tepees that was made from buffalo hide. So, they had to eat their tent. *Na xude the a. Na xude the tani ga.* That's how hard times they had.

And this one time, they come home abundantly. Plenty of dried buffalo. And when they left they planted their garden. In the fall when they come home, with that dried meat, here their garden was ready for reaping. Pumpkins, what have you. They had corn, everything. Everything turned out plentiful. They were happy. They were glad. They didn't know where to go to. Seemed though they ought to tell somebody, their happy feelings. So they got together. "We ought to do something. Give thanks. We got plenty. We're going to pull through the winter real good. All we got to do for fresh meat is to go out and hunt for it." So, it was discussed. It wasn't one day, it wasn't two days. It went on, and on. Finally they got it started. And they asked my clan to make that drum. By the Omaha, the nation. So it was my people that made the drum. Who made the songs, I never heard that. Maybe they did that too, because they had the drum.

So, everything was ready. Then they come to the day. It was still in the Fall. Everyday, everyday, until they got it together. Made them songs. Then they danced and celebrated. Back there, I guess they danced all night — one night. At least one night. All night, celebrated. Before they started, they told Him what they were going to do. Why? Because they were happy and they thanked Him for it, so they celebrated and they danced.

And there, they didn't say they were the first ones. They made it, and that was it. Created it. And that's the way I heard it. No one else heard it, but this man that saw them, it was entirely different. There was no ceremony. Everybody was dancing, women and all. And so – Winnebagos, our neighboring tribe, that land was ours, but the Omaha's gave it to them on account they come down too far and the Sioux got back behind them. Fought them. Was whipping them. They was going to get rid of that band, but they come to the Omahas for help. The Omahas helped them, and they shooed the Siouxs back home where they come from. And they said they were afraid to go home on account of the river. They'd have to stay on this side. They'd have to go through the Sioux land. And they were afraid. So, if you want to stay we will give you half of our reservation. *No^{n}de udo^n* [Good hearts]. You can be good to a certain extent, but they pulled that one too deep.

But they [Winnebago] say they are the first, the oldest [powwow]. That's what made me ask Old Man Turner. He didn't say "yes," he didn't say, "no." But I told him what I heard from my grandpa. My dad. They were talking about it. And I told him what I heard, and I said I've been telling my children that. Now, it seems I'm at the point that I've been lying, I guess. Winnebagos said they was the first ones... powwow. He didn't say, "no" or nothing. He said I'm his grandpa. He's an off-branch from the *Ko^{n}ze*, I guess He says, "*Tigo^{n}ho! Ithaite udo^n*. It's good that you're talking, he said... in doing your talking. He said that's good.

Even that name, *Huto^{n}ga* [Big Voice, Omaha name for the Winnebago], is quite a boaster. He said, "That's what they are, but," he said this, "it was given to them by the Omaha. And they gave it to the Sioux. And then the Pawnee." The fourth one [group to receive the powwow-type war dance], he didn't tell it. I don't know who it was. Maybe a neighboring tribe the Omaha gave to. So, that's one good history of the Omaha and that powwow. So, I lived on the Missouri, but I could tell you that much.

END TAPE

Appendix F
JACOB "ZAC" DRUM
July 15, 1992

Born June 21, 1928, Jacob is the son of Carrie Morris and Pete Drum. In the early 1990s Jacob resided with his wife and family in a home located on the Missouri River bottomland east of Macy. A noted singer of traditional Omaha songs, Jacob has served as head singer for many Omaha ceremonial gatherings. I had a nodding relationship with Jacob, but had never had the opportunity to sit and visit at length about any particular subject. Jacob was asked to participate in this study because earlier interviews with other Omaha elders elicited continual references to Carrie and Pete Drum as members of dance lodge organizations. Jacob's publicly recognized interest in the preservation and transmission of traditional Omaha songs suggested the potential for his knowing something about dance lodge activities. Because of my pre-existing clan relationship with his wife, I always used the term "Uncle" when speaking to Jacob. Following Auntie's untimely passing a few years after this project was completed, the relationship was re-evaluated so that I now address Jacob as "Father".The following interview took place in Jacob's rural home east of Macy, Nebraska.

Lodges east of Macy...

MR. AWAKUNI-SWETLAND: [consulting a photograph] That's supposed to be over at Silas Woods' place, just east of Macy, between the two bridges [on Highway 75], that cornfield out there.

MR. DRUM: Yeah, I remember this. Yeah, Silas Woods' place. Yeah, I remember [the lodge]. They had that there. But there was — the top part here was, you know, all caved in and rotted out. I don't know what year they put that up, you know. But it was run down. Oh, around '36, I think.

And there's a house over here, the Dan Walker place. It would be right south of Dan Walker's, down in the bottom here, right around in there.

MR. AWAKUNI-SWETLAND: Do you think that you would be able to walk over there today and probably stand on where that site was? Do you think it's still possible to find it that way?

MR. DRUM: Well, there's so many machinery and tractors went by there. [You] probably could get the general idea where it's at, see. But, it's not all the same, like I said. One time we had so much rain, like this year, and they just flooded all over that ground over there. That creek bed was just floating over everything. Them trees along the bank, there, they happen to just break loose and float down the water and stuck here and there after the water went down. So, that happened, too, you know.

Lodges south of Macy...

MR. AWAKUNI-SWETLAND: Are you familiar with any other dance lodges? Any other big structures like that around the reservation?

MR. DRUM: No, not that big. But the others down south, here, where my father used to participate at all the time, oh, the peoples lived down south, you know, country homes, they got together and just like making these hand games, and things like that, they got together and just like fund raising. They got to get their lumber and stuff, and everybody pitches in to volunteer to build that lodge up, down south. They had their own lodge, then, at that time. And when they got it set up and ready for it, and then there was no electric at the time. No electric going through. So, they had to use these bright lights, you know. Kind of kerosene lights. They hang them wherever they can get them up. Then they got some well outfit to dig them wells and horse tanks, there, so they can water their horses and keep that thing full. At that time everybody makes themselves at home, there, you know. Hitch the horses and feed them and tell them to rest up their horses.

MR. AWAKUNI-SWETLAND: Were you ever in that lodge down south?

MR. DRUM: Yeah. We used to participate in war dances and things like that when I was about as big as Michael, there [age 10-12]. We used to — My brother used to participate. And at that time they weren't no fancy dances, they were all traditionals.

MR. AWAKUNI-SWETLAND: Traditional dancers?

MR. DRUM: Yeah. You didn't see no fancy dancers until later years come up there. Those that wanted to dance fancy dances, they fixed their own outfits and start dancing fancy.

MR. AWAKUNI-SWETLAND: The lodge down south, did it have a name?

MR. DRUM: They were Little Skunks. *Mo^{n}gazhi^{n}ga*, they call them. Little Skunks.

MR. AWAKUNI-SWETLAND: And do you remember where that site was?

MR. DRUM: Yeah. Yeah. I remember where that site was. At that time that road wasn't going straight west [from highway 75]. There was no road there at all. Just an old wagon trail, you know. No cars. About '36 when they started building these cars, you know, that's when it's coming in. I remember my uncle, Joseph Drum, was the first Omaha Indian to own a new car, 1936 V-8 Ford. I don't know, maybe the Model T's come before then or '24 or something like that, you know. But he was the first person to have that new car.

MR. AWAKUNI-SWETLAND: Is that the lodge that sat down next to the Warren Davis place?

MR. DRUM: Yeah, over the hill there. There was Warren Davis there and there was a guy from Kansas named John Lasley. These Lasley boys there, the grandsons, Henry Lasley. That's his son, you know. That's where these Lasley boys come from, you know. That's their grandfather. Them boys, they lived a little ways from there, in the square house. Then, Old Man Alec Esau, was over the hill from there, kind of southwest, down below there. Then another house, Old Man Henry Grant lived there. Then right south of Warren Davis they were Dick — Tecumseh Dick lived there. And Henry Dick got that new home there, now. Of course, he's deceased now, but — Then further on, you know, up the draw there Morgan Stabler and them others lived there.

So, there were quite a few Omaha tribes down that way, too. I think that was — at the time, they were making good homes and lived pretty good. But they kind of have a hard times, sometimes, to go to town and nothing to drive or no team or nothing, well they had to walk for their groceries at that time. But today you look at it and being out in the country it's better, you know. It's better to be in town and you enjoy your life in the open air and the fresh air and all of that.

Now, everything's kind of — like I say, the last time you were here, that our ways — traditional ways — are all going to leave us. There ain't much of it left, now, as you take in dances and things like that, like maybe the emcee says, "Well, we're going to have our traditional ways of doing things. Everything is going to be our way." But times that goes in some other tribe's ways, you know, they use that.

Just like where one boy I was talking to here a couple, three days ago, named Richard — Richard St. Cyr, here — Richard Poffabiddy, his name. And he's part Omaha and Comanche over there. He said they having a powwow all around there, Kiowas and Comanches and other tribes. Now the Kiowas were having their powwow. They're doing it over there, now, he says, but they've got closed gates. No other tribe can get in there to participate or help out, because the Kiowas don't want no — don't want their traditional ways to go to different tribes. And when they go over there to see their dance, why that's a Kiowa way and they didn't like that, he said. So, they didn't want other tribes to come in to participate, because they were taking too much of their ways away from them. And very little that Kiowas do [are] their ways, he said. So, that's the way it is, I guess today here.

Like I say, myself, I really don't take in any of these dances anymore. That's all I can remember about my father. Of course, he helps out everybody. He run the powwow and he does his best to help people at the time. And he's a good talker. And he knows just about what to say when he gets before the peoples and explain things to them in the right way and not to get after peoples or tell them anything. Just all his words, whatever he says it's all thanks. Thank you words to them. And that's the kind of a person he was. Maybe that's how come he left so soon, you know. His time had come up and leave this mother earth. He was a young man at the time. I think he died when he was 51 years old.

And along in the '40s he done a lot of things for them — for the peoples he had tried to help. Whatever they asked him, he'll do his best to help them out in that way. He never turned them down. He made a lot of efforts to run peyote meetings, whatever has to be done. Although even if he has to walk with us children, we had to walk, walk with him wherever it's going to be, we were there the day before, because you can't make it in a day. It will take you a whole day to walk. You have to walk quite a ways, 10, 20 miles, that's a long walk. Especially climbing these hills, you know. So, we always make our ways to get there the day before and stay with a family overnight.

But he run that lodge and he named all — what the lodge was going to be named for and all of that. He had a nice organization going at the time. Everybody helps. Everybody is willing to go for this hand games and war dances and stuff like that.

MR. AWAKUNI-SWETLAND: Do you remember who else was in that group with him?

MR. DRUM: Yeah, there was quite a few of them. Like, George Mitchell, Dave Mitchell, Roy Mitchell, Ernest Smith, Clyde Hallowell, Sam Harlan, Alec Walker, Henry Walker, Stewart Walker, Fred Baxter, Frank Baxter, George Blackbird, Robert Smith, Henry Lovejoy, Henry Grant, Alec Esau. There was a quite a bunch.

MR. AWAKUNI-SWETLAND: All *Mog^{n}azhi^{n}ga.*

MR. DRUM: All *Mo^{n}gazhi^{n}ga.* He had a big organization. At that time the man's have the meetings or visit and talk to one another and talk about, you know, what's going to take place. They don't allow the ladies to inter-fere in their business. They put ladies, maybe in the kitchen. If these guys have a meeting outside, the ladies would be in the house. At the time they don't let the ladies interfere in the men's business, what they're talking about. And the same way the ladies, though, when they have some kind of meeting, they don't allow the men in at that time.

Decline of lodges...

[Later in time] they take care of them [lodges], but they have their livestock in there. They go in there and the livestock is there. At the time the fences were not up. Herds run through here and there, wherever they can pick up what they want to eat. Livestock get in there and maybe, I don't know, maybe the flies bothered them too much, or whatever. They would just run in those lodges and stay there and make a big mess. And it died down. Everything kind of died down quite a bit, then. After livestock got in there, why, nobody seemed to care to get in there and clean it up.

But Horse Head Lodge, you know, they tried the best, you know. Even my uncle, Tom Morris, fixed it one time, patched it up for them and they used it for a while. Then after they kind of — Well, it depends, you know. The groups — organization selects the officers. And it seemed like the officers are pretty slow getting around, making headway. They're not lively as the first one was, you know. It seemed like they'd push it onto themselves and let somebody else, you know, make suggestions to do this, do that. And the leader will sit back and let them go the way they want to. Sometimes they don't have meetings and talk about this and maybe we should get out there and fix that lodge up, and maybe get fund raising going, things like that. But they don't do it.

After that Horse Head Lodge went down, well they built kind of an arbor-like over there where Tyler Walker used to live. They had one there, at Horse Head Lodge. They built one there, you know. I don't know where they got that lumber, but they said they picked up some lumber from the old run-down homes and things like that. They set a post, you know, in each one of them corners, just post here and there and they had nothing but cardboard things on there. Of course, the roof, you know, they had that tarpaper on there so it won't leak when it rains. Which they can keep that big lodge going. It was pretty steady at that time, too, all the two-by-fours standing good, clear around it. Some of the bracing up on the roof, there, was kind of, you know, splitting here and there, but always could replace them or patch them up.

Well, that's the way it kind of turned out to be, you know. You sit there and think about it. The president of the group has got to keep moving. That's how my father came up with, you know. That's why he was in there all that time. Every time they have elections, they have voting going on, why, they always put him back in there to keep things going for them. And that's what everything went really good for the people. And they liked him in that way.

Whenever each organization, like to, you know, play hand game, they play against one another. Like the Horse Head Lodge, why they want to challenge the Little Skunks, they call them. Either way, they go down there. They have their own singing groups. They have two drums. The Skunks have their own drums and the Horse Heads have their own drums. Whenever they had to hide the stones, why, you know, they'd go back and forth, singing, going back and forth like that.

MR. AWAKUNI-SWETLAND: You're singing for your own side?

MR. DRUM: Yeah, singing for your own organization, like that. And every organization was like that at the time, Wind Lodge and all of the organizations, gathered here on the reservation. And they have their own singing groups. One time they asked me to organize the Little Skunks, bring them back up, because they left everything to me and my dad, "You're going to have to take over when I'm gone, and all that, so you just as well learn when you're young, learn your ways of doing things here. When I'm gone, why, you're going to take the same track here, what I'm doing. Maybe one of these days the peoples will come and ask you something, like you today, and ask you to reorganize this group. Maybe they'll be all split up. Maybe they'll be all gone, back to mother earth. And maybe you can reorganize

young brothers and reorganize. Maybe you can do that, keep this going."
But I never tried to do that, you know. Some of them asked me, some of
the old members still living, like George Mitchell, some of them asked me
if I can reorganize them. I didn't pay any attention.

As I see it myself, you know, it's hard work. It seems like there's no time
for you to sit around and visit around. You have to be thinking of something for them to get things started. Like this time of the year, you know,
everything is — powwow is coming up and you have to make fund raising
for going somewhere, fill you cars, put gas in, eating and lodging and all of
that. I didn't want to take a big responsibility. I figured I'm all right, just
the way I am trying to help out this way, you know. Whatever I remember
and whatever my dad done.

Lodge features described...

MR. AWAKUNI-SWETLAND: When people gathered to have a dance, or
let's say a hand game, inside the lodge —here's the lodge, here's that east
side. The door is on the east side. What held the roof up? Was there a ring
of poles, or center poles or —

MR. DRUM: Center pole.

MR. AWAKUNI-SWETLAND: There was a center pole?

MR. DRUM: Yeah, center pole. Then them two-by-fours go right up to a
center pole, like that. Yeah, like that. There were big braces right in the center here where these poles could lay on, see.

MR. AWAKUNI-SWETLAND: There were braces on the poles?

MR. DRUM: Yeah, there were braces on the pole, there.

MR. AWAKUNI-SWETLAND: For the rafters. Windows?

MR. DRUM: They didn't have no windows, but just this one here. I seen
windows on that old Silas Wood. There were windows on it. But like Horse
Head Lodge and Little Skunk Lodge and Wind Lodge, they didn't have no
windows in them. They just one way getting in there and one way getting
out.

MR. AWAKUNI-SWETLAND: And was it dirt floor?

MR. DRUM: Yeah, dirt floor.

MR. AWAKUNI-SWETLAND: And where did the singers sit?

MR. DRUM: Right besides the poles, here. They build their own benches there. At the time we didn't have — they didn't have those folding chairs and they built those benches high enough for the peoples to sit.

MR. AWAKUNI-SWETLAND: All the way around?

MR. DRUM: All the way around and there was no folding chairs or nothing at the time. Maybe there were, but I never — because all I can remember is them benches there they build so high, maybe as high as a chair. They put poles in them and tacked the boards right on top.

MR. AWAKUNI-SWETLAND: Oh, just a post and a plank?

MR. DRUM: Yeah, put a post about that big and set them inside the ground and then put that plank on top. There was no cement blocks at the time. The singers were in the center, there.

MR. AWAKUNI-SWETLAND: If you were playing a hand game against another group, did both drums sit side-by-side?

MR. DRUM: No, they, like this group here would be on this side, the north side, and this group would be on this side. All right, they have their seats opposite from each other's drums. They'd be sitting on the sidelines or corner of the house. But it was sitting opposite of them, singing for their group.

MR. AWAKUNI-SWETLAND: But if it was a dance or something, they'd have...

MR. DRUM: Yeah, they'd have to sit at the middle. At that time there was no drum at the sidelines, no such thing.

MR. AWAKUNI-SWETLAND: And the *nudo^{n}ho^{n}ga*, the head people, where would they be sitting, one's who were score keepers?

MR. DRUM: Well, the score keepers would be on the west side. Yeah. Always west.

MR. AWAKUNI-SWETLAND: Did they cook or have any heating inside?

MR. DRUM: No, they cook outside. They have wood burning grills and things.

MR. AWAKUNI-SWETLAND: What about wintertime when it was cold, was there any way to keep that warm in there?

MR. DRUM: Well, wintertime, probably burned wood. I remember they put a stovepipe through Horse Head — I mean, Little Skunks' roof. They put a heater there, a wood heater, a great big heater.

MR. AWAKUNI-SWETLAND: Do you remember where it sat?

MR. DRUM: It was sitting on the north side of this door, here. A pretty good area, here. They had a big heater there and they put that chimney right about —

MR. AWAKUNI-SWETLAND: [consulting the Silas Wood photograph] Does this show a chimney at all?

MR. DRUM: Yeah, one of them do.

MR. AWAKUNI-SWETLAND: Yeah, that shows it.

MR. DRUM: Yeah, this one here.

MR. AWAKUNI-SWETLAND: A stovepipe.

MR. DRUM: Yeah, that's where they put them. This one here is right up in the middle, Silas Wood.

MR. AWAKUNI-SWETLAND: And then that Horse Head Lodge has a brick chimney.

MR. DRUM: A brick chimney.

MR. AWAKUNI-SWETLAND: Right up the middle.

MR. DRUM: Yeah, right up the middle. But they just — I think they just put it that way because I never did see them use any heater there. When they did, well they put it like this [indicating off to one side].

Other Groups and Lodges...

MR. AWAKUNI-SWETLAND: Do you remember — Let's see, Big Crazies, *Gtho^{n}thi^{n}to^{n}ga*, do you remember hearing of that organization, the Big Crazies? Are they the ones that used the Horse Head Lodge?

MR. DRUM: Well, they're the ones. Yeah, that's the group. Because *Gtho^{n}thi^{n}to^{n}ga*, that's them. They named themselves in English, Horse Head Lodge. That's what the building — this building is named, the Horse Head Lodge.

MR. AWAKUNI-SWETLAND: What about the *Gtho^{n}thi^{n}zhiga*, Little Crazies? Ever hear of them?

MR. DRUM: Yeah. Part of them organizations, my father's members joined that club to keep that organization going. They're down south, too. They used the same lodge over there. So, they are part of my dad's organizations members are in that. And some of the other groups get in on that. So, they use the same lodging down there, the *Mo^{n}gazhi^{n}ga* Lodge. But later on, why, they kind of —later years, you know, I don't know how many years they've been together but kind of went into this Little Skunk Lodge. Why is it they have two names: Little Skunks and *Gtho^{n}thi^{n}zhi^{n}ga*, why is it we having it. One split, you know, kind of names. So why is it that we shouldn't have one name. So we're going to go into the Little Skunks. So they all did. So that *Gtho^{n}thi^{n}zhi^{n}ga* kinda washed up.

MR. AWAKUNI-SWETLAND: Let's see, do you remember another group, *Waho^{n}thi^{n}ge*?

MR. DRUM: Well, just lately. They're organized. They're in Omaha, too, but around here I never — My dad always said that there is a group of that. I remember him saying he named them, that group in Omaha, that *Waho^{n}thi^{n}ge*, they call it. My dad gave them that name, *Waho^{n}thi^{n}ge*. They organized in Omaha, the group there. They called him to ask him a name. They didn't have a name, so he went over there and told them that — he named that group, *Waho^{n}nthi^{n}ge*, but he said there is a group way back in his young days there were *Waho^{n}thi^{n}ge* here in reservation. They were going pretty strong at the time I guess. He didn't say how they broke up or how they didn't get together any more. But he said that much, and I heard him that much. Ever since then, *Waho^{n}thi^{n}ge* had that name there, in the city. Even made song for them, I guess, but I never did hear that song.

MR. AWAKUNI-SWETLAND: Did you ever hear who was in the old *Waho^{n}thi^{n}ge* around here?

MR. DRUM: No. Like I say, he didn't mention anybody in that time, you know. I would remember it if he had said that. I would remember the names of who would be the oldest of that group. But he didn't name them. All he said was, *Waho^{n}thi^{n}ge* were here.

MR. AWAKUNI-SWETLAND: There's another group I heard of, *Ixasto^n*, Opossums?

MR. DRUM: Yeah, there was a group like that. Emily Parker was one of them, her father, Old Man John Kemp —them Kemp brothers, there's three of them, let's see, Silas, Orson, John. Old Man Dave Miller, they're the ones down southwest, there, where Emily lives, all along in that area. They call themselves *Ixasto^n*. That's a little group there, a small group. They play among themselves. Of course, whenever they call on them, well, they probably, you know, go challenge whoever is calling them. But it was a small group going there. But that was a long — them groups hang down a long time until everybody, you know, kinda dying out.

MR. AWAKUNI-SWETLAND: Another group Emily mentioned, White Riders, *Agthi^{n}Ska*, they were called. She said she thought that Henry Turner and some of the *Gtho^{n}thi^{n}to^{n}ga* were in that.

MR. DRUM: Yeah.

MR. AWAKUNI-SWETLAND: But she didn't know anything else about them, White Riders.

MR. DRUM: Yeah, I heard about them, but I didn't quite get the details. I just heard about them. There were groups, you know. Nobody hardly mentioned about them.

MR. AWAKUNI-SWETLAND: The last group I heard about was *Si Sabe*.

MR. DRUM: Yeah, they're west.

MR. AWAKUNI-SWETLAND: Uh-huh.

MR. DRUM: Blackfoot, *Si Sabe*. Now, they were a big organization, too. They had that lodge out there. They used Wind Lodge. Yeah, they're all in one, you know. The oldest was Wind Lodge and they're all kind of dying out, like I say. Well, these organizations come in there, they're kind of carrying on, but they used that Wind Lodge, *Si Sabe*. Right where that Wind Lodge is, I suppose Tom took you over there. You go on that road and then you go up on top of that hill and you turn south and they used to have big powwows there, too, up in that ridge that kind of sloped down this way. I don't know how they had powwow .

MR. AWAKUNI-SWETLAND: The Wind Lodge sat down here on the —

here's that creek that runs and this is Macy over here. You go up that road. Here's that road.

MR. DRUM: Yeah, going north and south, up on that hill. Right after you come south, why just all along in here. They used to have powwows there, yeah, right in there.

MR. AWAKUNI-SWETLAND: Did you ever hear about somebody having a merry-go-round over there, a steam merry-go-round?

MR. DRUM: A steam merry-go-round? Yeah, I've heard of that but I can't remember the name now. It's been a long time. Somebody had a merry-to-round there for, you know —

MR. AWAKUNI-SWETLAND: I heard it was one them Cayou, either Lee or Fred or somebody like that.

MR. DRUM: Lee Cayou, yeah, I think that was him. Lee Cayou had that merry-go-round.

MR. AWAKUNI-SWETLAND: Let's see, Harry Lyons lived over here somewhere didn't he? He was over on this side of the road somewhere, across from the Wind Lodge?

MR. DRUM: Yeah.

MR. AWAKUNI-SWETLAND: where the McCauleys lived?

MR. DRUM: McCauleys — Jim McCauley used to live there. Lyons, that's Old Lady McCauley's parents.

MR. AWAKUNI-SWETLAND: Jim McCauley was married to one of them girls.

MR. DRUM: Yeah, one of them girls at that time.

MR. AWAKUNI-SWETLAND: And then there was the Robinson place over here —

MR. DRUM: Yeah, over the hill. East side, right near the road, there. George Robinson. And there was Albert Robinson just where you go up this first hill, down below there, right down back over there, back in there. Yeah, that's where Robinson used to live there. And then George lived here and Alec Black lived next to him. George Robinson, Alex Black, Boots

Robinson — Newton Robinson — was on the corner.

George Robinson lived there.

MR. AWAKUNI-SWETLAND: Who is the one they called Spark Plug?

MR. DRUM: That's him.

MR. AWAKUNI-SWETLAND: George?

MR. DRUM: George. Spark Plug. Over where Newton lives, that road, if you go around that turn, up the hill, going around that turn that little road goes over there, that's where John Robinson lived, back in that grove. Then there's a White man lived right next to him, name Leinhart. Then right across the road here, across the ditch, over in here Alfred Blackbird lived there. Then Fish Walker, that's where Judy Ike lives in that place, now, at the Alfred Blackbird place.

MR. AWAKUNI-SWETLAND: Something I have been noticing is that in those days the countryside was full of people. There was people out there all, and some of them were kind of old, you know. Nowadays, all the old people live up on the hill at Macy and the few people that live out here are younger. So, it would have been easy back in those days to kind of organize.

MR. DRUM: Yeah, kind of organize. That's what I say. You sit and think about those homes, you know, how close they can live, you know. It's a lot easier and quiet and more enjoyable and alive, all this fresh air you're getting. Just like I say, you have — if you don't have nothing to ride into town, well you've just got to start hiking the first thing in the morning and get your groceries and get on home. That's about it. Times that you have to walk a long ways. There's no car that's going to come around and give you a ride, you know, because there wasn't any. In them days, that's what I say, you know, it's good to live out in the country like that.

These neighbors that we put down, you know, they visit one another. Like these homes right there, this home and that home and that home, they all bunch up sometimes and visit in the evenings. And get together. That's how they brings things up, you know, maybe they'd talk about this and that and then pretty soon, well, hey, why don't we try that. Why don't we just go and do that. That's how they get the ideas of doing things.

And very, very, very few ever talked English. All Omaha words when they talked, nothing but Omaha. Today, you have to talk English to your children. They don't understand you if you talk Indian to them, that's how come I know a lot of things, you know. I'm around more Indian than *Waxe*. I'm not much of an English speaker, either. I know a lot of my Indian ways, the *Umo^{n}ho^n* ways. I talk *Umo^{n}ho^n*. I say a lot of good things in there, but those that wouldn't, aren't understanding what I'm saying. Today you have to translate your words, you know. When you say something in Indian, then you come back and explain it over to them English.

Yeah, that's what I do and I'm kind of getting up into the age where I can sit and think what my parents told me. They said, one of these days you're going to think back and realize a lot of things, but we'll be gone and you won't have nobody to turn back to or ask anybody. Because they'll be gone. They'll be gone forward.

Omaha shinny game...

MR. AWAKUNI-SWETLAND: Even when we're — when I've been talking with people about lodges and groups and stuff, usually, you know, they'll bring up shinny game as an example. Shinny game was a big thing back in those days, but most of the people I've talked to, they don't think you could play shinny nowadays. Everybody gets mad right away and beat one another up with shinny sticks. We're all different from the old days. We don't get along like we used to.

MR. DRUM: Yeah, they have that every Sunday, my dad used to organize. Just like we were talking about, these clubs, members, they play against one another. They just no mixed up in there. You've got to belong to a group to be in that game. Or, you've got to be a member of the group to get in that game. They play those — they play one group and the other group takes on the winner and so on like that, challenge one another. All of the good times they have, throughout the afternoons.

MR. AWAKUNI-SWETLAND: What kind of the year did they play?

MR. DRUM: Oh, they play along in July, this time of the year. But whenever, from the month of July into August, whenever an organization wants to challenge this and that, why they get together and call the man that's running it. They need permission from the guy that's running it, they need to ask him in the right way if they can play. To go ahead and manage it for them.

MR. AWAKUNI-SWETLAND: A Man-in-charge kind of thing?

MR. DRUM: Yeah. Because he runs that, see. That's our ways and our clan. That's why we're the seventh one, all of the rest of the clans are way up in the air, but we're way down here. Like these powwow times, they call upon me to say an invocation, I can't do it. All these storms and rain and all of that, they believe in their old clan and the ways. They believe in it. That's just the way it is. My dad run that for many years, too. It used to be good. There was no fighting or nothing, no arguments. He'd have two sticks up on the west and the east side and that ball would go right in between them. Tey'd have a couple of guys sitting behind them — in front of them sticks to keep that ball from — just like a skate hockey game.

MR. AWAKUNI-SWETLAND: How far apart were they?

MR. DRUM: Oh, they were about six feet apart. They cut those poles, oh, about that big [indicating a diameter with his hands] and stick them down and he'd cut the bark off them so you could see.

MR. AWAKUNI-SWETLAND: Four-inch poles. How tall were they, very tall?

MR. DRUM: No, about four, about like that, three or four feet. Put it down about two feet down.

MR. AWAKUNI-SWETLAND: How long was the playing field?

MR. DRUM: Oh, shoot, you go clear across the field. It was quite — almost a quarter of a mile, I think. At that time. Because that field was real wide, open, everybody. No matter how hard you hit that ball, you were going to have to get it. There was no sidelines or nothing, just open field. Everybody runs after that ball. It ain't like basketball lines, and things like that, outside a ball, I think that —

MR. AWAKUNI-SWETLAND: So the ball could get knocked over where spectators are watching and you guys could plow into the spectators, huh?

MR. DRUM: Not that bad, though. The spectators all out on the road. Cars — at that time they had cars. People would drive cars and there were old Chevys, whatever, back in the '20s. Yeah, I kept that ball for quite a while and it got away. My uncle Buddy [Gilpin] said to bring that ball over and he'd put it in a museum but I said, no, don't do that. I've kept that ball for a long time. My dad passed away and he didn't authorize anybody to take this ball and carry on, I'm the only one and why should I put it in the museum. It don't belong there. But it got away. I don't know where it went to. We've moved around so much.

MR. AWAKUNI-SWETLAND: You said he made it out of boot leather?

MR. DRUM: Boot leather, yeah.

MR. AWAKUNI-SWETLAND: Kind of oblong?

MR. DRUM: Yeah, that boot used to be this tall, you know. They laced them where the side is, cut both of them out. And then he soaked it with grease, oil. He left it about a couple of days and that leather was just soft, but it was greasy. Punched a hole in it and he laced it up after it dried out, you know, real soft. I guess they know what they were doing at that time. By the time you stuff cotton and laced it up and dried it up some more. Round — sort of like that.

MR. AWAKUNI-SWETLAND: About six inch around.

MR. DRUM: With padding in them. And then they make them sticks, you know, burn them. Put wires on them and them put them in live ashes and take them barks off and you have a shinny club of your own.

MR. AWAKUNI-SWETLAND: How thick?

MR. DRUM: They're about that big around. Depends how big you want to make them.

MR. AWAKUNI-SWETLAND: About like an ax handle?

MR. DRUM: A little smaller. Some make them out of willows, pretty good-sized willows. Some make them out of small oaks, you know, them new little trees. Wherever you can bend them, you know.

MR. AWAKUNI-SWETLAND: Did everybody make their own stick?

MR. DRUM: Yeah, everybody carry their own. Then they let them guys come this way with their sticks and throw them in the middle. It's not like a group that's going to take on this group or that group. They say you guys get together and whoever is going to pick these sticks up, he's going to throw them oN one side, so many to one side and throw some more on that side. He tell them, you guys mark your sticks so you know which one is yours. So, they do that, you know, tie a red handkerchief or whatever they've got. Then they bunch the sticks up, and then he'd go over and pick up a hand full and throw them to one side and a hand full to that side until they were all gone. And everybody start hunting for their sticks. They know which side they are going to play on, see. Your stick is on this side, why, you're going to play against this side. Same thing.

Uou make a little hill for that ball, like that and set that ball right on top of there. He'd have two guys put the sticks right next to the ball like that, ready to knock it off. All they do is push that off and which way they fall, the ball falls, they don't hit it like that from the beginning. They just push it off. But he tells them, in Indian, "Whenever this ball falls over, you step back and you step back, so the next guy could pick it up and hit it easy. When it gets way out there, no matter how much you swing that bat — club, watch out, the guy next to you." He talks to them guys and everything goes along good. That's the only time they say "*Tabe gadaba.* Indians, *tabe o^n gadabai ga*. He tells them, "*Tabe o^n gadabai gaho*." Well, you put that ball on top of that little hill. But whoever makes the goal, why, they bring that ball back and start all over.

MR. AWAKUNI-SWETLAND: Which teams wins? How do you win a game?

MR. DRUM: Well, just like I said, they're all mixed. They don't go by just certain teams, everybody play mixed. But if you are going to play the Wind Lodge and you're going to play the Horse Head Lodge, they don't much call them sticks. That's another way of doing it. So, he put two guys over here — two guys here. This guy here stands here and another one stands over there — and this guy has a guy here and another one stands over here, in four directions, the four winds. According to that, the four winds. All right, he puts that ball on top of there and this guy standing over here and this guy standing over here and there's two guys, the guy standing here, whichever — okay, they just drop that ball to one side, or this guy standing here will have to hit it back. Then they know which team is against one another, like Wind Lodge and Horse Head Lodge. So, they play it all different ways, you know. But if you get guys [who are] all mixed guys, it's interesting, you know.

We'd just sit there and watch. We weren't big enough or old enough to play. But we watched. There was no trouble, there was no alcoholic or nothing. There might be home brews, but, you know, they dare to come in. You watched them that close.

MR. AWAKUNI-SWETLAND: They decided how many points they were going to play for?

MR. DRUM: Yeah, like 20 games.

MR. AWAKUNI-SWETLAND: Twenty games?

MR. DRUM: Twenty games. And if they're going to challenge another group, a group against a group, why they go to 12, 12 rounds.

MR. AWAKUNI-SWETLAND: Until some — They put the ball on the hill 12 times and whoever has the most scores?

MR. DRUM: Yeah, scores.

MR. AWAKUNI-SWETLAND: So, it might be seven to five, or eight to four?

MR. DRUM: Something like that.

MR. AWAKUNI-SWETLAND: Oh, okay. Besides your dad, who else in your clan could referee them things?

MR. DRUM: The Gilpins.

MR. AWAKUNI-SWETLAND: The Gilpins.

MR. DRUM: Lee Gilpin, Isaac, Joe, Buddy, Lawrence, we're same clan. We were about the only ones. There were a lot of *Tapa* [Deer Clan], a bunch of them, the *Ho^{n}ga* [Leader Buffalo Clan]. That's the most of the clan there, two clans at most today. But I don't believe these younger generations don't even know what clans they are. They think they are *Waxe* [White Men]. They think they ain't got no clans. Even *Waxe*'s have, you know, they're like clans, you know. They go by their ways. I notice that people in New York and nationality, and what nationalities are. They know. It's just like that.

END TAPE

Bibliography

Amgwert, Patty *The Omaha People: The Teachers Guide for an Encounter Kit for the Omaha Tribe.* Lincoln: University of Nebraska State Museum 1990[?].

Anderson, John A., Henry W. Hamilton, and Jean Tyree Hamilton, *The Sioux of the Rosebud: A History in Pictures,* Norman: University of Oklahoma Press, 1971.

Bernstein, Alison R. *American Indians and World War II: A New Era in Indian Affairs.* Norman: University of Oklahoma Press, 1991.

Blackbird, Elmer et al. *Omaha Youth Math and Science Activities.* Lincoln: Nebraska Math & Science Initiative, 1994.

Boughter, Judith A. *Betraying the Omaha Nation, 1790–1916,* Norman: University of Oklahoma Press, 1998.

Callahan, Alice Anne. *The Osage Ceremonial Dance I'n-Lon-Schka,* Norman: University of Oklahoma Press, 1990.

Cobb, Stephen, Hollis D. Stabler, Kathy Vander Werff, editors, *La-ta-we-sah (Woman of the Bird Clan): Her Poetry and Prose.* Macy, Nebraska: Macy School Press, 1989.

Densmore, Frances. *Pawnee Music,* Smithsonian Institution, Bureau of American Ethnology Bulletin 93. Washington, DC: Government Printing Office, 1929

Dorsey, James Owen. *Omaha Sociology.* Third Annual Report, Bureau of American Ethnology (1881–1882). Washington, DC: Government Printing Office, 1884.

—. Omaha Dwellings, Furniture, and Implements. Thirteen Annual Report. Bureau of American Ethnology (1891–1896). Washington, D. C. : Government Printing Office, 1896.

The egiha Language. U.S. Geographical and Geological Survey of the Rocky Mountain Region, Contributions to North American Ethnology. Washington, DC: Government Printing Office, 1890.

Fixico, Donald L. *Termination and Relocation: Federal Indian Policy, 1945–1960.* Albuquerque: University of New Mexico Press, 1986.

Fletcher, Alice Cunningham. (Editor) *Memorial of the Members of the Omaha Tribe of Indians for a Grant of Land in Severalty.* 47th Congress, 1st Session, Senate Miscellaneous Documents, no. 31, 1882.

"Omaha Indian Allotments, 1882–1883." Ledger book, 1884. Great Plains Art Collection, Center for Great Plains Studies, University of Nebraska-Lincoln.
Historical Sketch of the Omaha Tribe of Indians in Nebraska. Washington, DC: Judd and Detweiler Printers, 1885.

Lands in Severalty to Indians, Illustrated by Experiences with the Omaha Tribe. Salem, MA: Salem Press, 1885.

"Personal Studies of Indian Life: Politics and 'Pipe-Dancing'." *The Century Magazine* 45(1893):441–455.

Fletcher, Alice Cunningham and Francis La Flesche. *The Omaha Tribe.* Twenty-Seventh Annual Report, Bureau of American Ethnology (1905–1906). Washington, DC: Government Printing Office, 1911.

Fortune, Reo F. *Omaha Secret Societies.* New York: A. M. S. Press, 1969.

Fowler, Loretta. *Shared Symbols, Contested Meanings: Gros Ventre Culture and History, 1778–1984,* Ithaca: Cornell University Press, 1987.

Green, Albert Lamborn. "The Language and Customs of a Nearly Extinct Nation of Ancient Quivera Whose Component Bands Still Survive and Are Known as the Otoes, Iowas, and Missouris." A. L. Green Manuscript Collection, Nebraska State Historical Society, Lincoln, 1939.

Gurcke, Karl. *Bricks and Brickmaking.* Moscow: University of Idaho Press, 1987.

Howard, James H. *The Ponca Tribe.* Smithsonian Institution, Bureau of American Ethnology Bulletin 195. Washington, DC: Government Printing Office, 1965.

Jensen, Richard E., R. Eli Paul, and John E. Carter. *Eyewitness at Wounded Knee.* Lincoln: University of Nebraska Press, 1991.

Kappler, Charles. *Indian Affairs: Laws and Treaties,* Volume I (Laws); Volume II (Treaties). Washington, DC: Government Printing Office, 1904.

La Flesche, Francis. *The Middle Five: Indian Schoolboys of the Omaha Tribe.* (originally published in 1900). Lincoln: University of Nebraska Press, 1963.

La Flesche Family Papers, Lincoln: Nebraska State Historical Society, MS2026. [1895?]

Lee, Dorothy Sara and Maria La Vigna, editors. *Omaha Indian Music: Historical Recordings from the Fletcher/La Flesche Collection,* American Folklife Center. Washington, DC: Library of Congress, 1985.

Liberty, Margot. "Population Trends Among Present-day Omaha Indians." *Plains Anthropologist* 20 (August 1975):225–230.

Longwell, A. R. "Lands of the Omaha Indians."M.A. Thesis, Department of Geography, University of Nebraska-Lincoln, 1961.

Mark, Joan. *A Stranger in Her Native Land: Alice Fletcher and the American Indians.* Lincoln: University of Nebraska Press, 1988.

McEvoy, Fredrick Dean. "A Thesis: Reservation Settlement Patterns of the Omaha Indians, 1854–1930." Honors Thesis, Department of Anthropology, University of Nebraska-Lincoln, 1963.

Mead, Margaret. *The Changing Culture of an Indian Tribe.* New York: Columbia University Press, 1932.

Native American Public Broadcasting Consortium. *Return of the Sacred Pole,* 30 minute video. Lincoln: Native American Public Broadcasting Consortium, 1990.

Nebraska ETV Network. *Dancing to Give Thanks,* 30 minute video. Lincoln: Nebraska ETV Network, 1988.

Neihardt, John G. A Political Coup at Little Omaha, *IN* The Ancient Memory and Other Stories, edited by Hilda Neihardt Petri. Lincoln: University of Nebraska Press, 1991.

Omaha Tribe of Nebraska. "190th Umo[n]Ho[n] Nation Harvest Celebration"

(Souvenir Program), Macy: Omaha Tribe of Nebraska, 1994,

O'Shea, John M. and John Ludwickson. *Archaeology and Ethnohistory of the Omaha Indians: The Big Village Site.* Lincoln: University of Nebraska Press, 1992.

Painter, Edward. "Omaha Indian Allotments, 1871." Ledger book. Microfilm RG508, Roll No. 120, Nebraska State Historical Society, Lincoln, Nebraska.

Painter, Orrin C. *William Painter and His Father Dr. Edward Painter: Sketches and Reminiscences.* Baltimore, MD: The Arundel Press, 1914.

Prucha, Francis Paul. *The Great Father: The United States Government and the American Indian.* Lincoln: University of Nebraska Press, 1984).

Ridington, Robin and Dennis Hastings. *Blessing for a Long Time: The Sacred Pole of the Omaha Tribe.* Lincoln: University of Nebraska Press, 1997.

Royce, Charles. *Indian Land Cessions in the United States.* Extract from the Eighteenth Annual Report, Bureau of American Ethnology. Washington, DC: Government Printing Office, 1900.

Scherer, Mark R. *Imperfect Victories: The Legal Tenacity of the Omaha Tribe, 1945–1995* Lincoln: University of Nebraska Press, 1999.

Sorkin, Alan A. *American Indians and Federal Aid.* Washington, DC: Brookings Institute, 1971.

Standingwater, Steven. "People of the Smokey Waters: the Omahas." Macy, Nebraska: n.p., 1970.

Stewart, Omer C. *Peyote Religion: A History.* Norman: University of Oklahoma Press, 1987.

Swetland, Mark J. "Make-Believe White-Men" and the Omaha Land Allotments of 1871–1900 *Great Plains Research* 4.2 (August 1994): 201–236.

"Aspect of Omaha Land Allotments, 1855–1910: With Reference to a Series of Three Maps." Typescript in the author's possession, 1992.

"A Few Words Concerning the Fireplace at the Lincoln Indian Center, 1100 Military Road, Lincoln, Nebraska." Typescript in the author's possession, 1985.

United States. *Annual Report of the Commissioner of Indian Affairs.* Washington,

DC: Government Printing Office, 1859, 1861–2, 1864–5, 1867, 1869, 1871–2, 1875–9, 1881–9, 1891–5, 1897, 1899, 1921–6, 1930, 1932, 1939–41, 1943–45.

Department of the Interior, Office of Indian Affairs, *Constitution and Bylaws of the Omaha Tribe of Nebraska*. Washington, DC: Government Printing Office, 1936.

Department of the Interior, Office of Indian Affairs, *Corporate Charter of the Omaha Tribe of Nebraska*. Washington, DC: Government Printing Office, 1936.

Eighteenth Decennial Census of the United States, 1960 Census of Population. Volume 1, Characteristics of the Population, Part A Number of Inhabitants. Washington, DC: Government Printing Office, 1961.

Nineteenth Decennial Census of the United States, 1970 Census of Population. Volume 1, Characteristics of the Population, Part 29 Nebraska. Washington, DC: Government Printing Office, 1973.

1980 Census of Population. Volume 1, Characteristics of the Population, Chapter B General Population Characteristics, Part 29 Nebraska. PC80-1-B29. Washington, DC: Government Printing Office, 1982.

1990 Census of Population. General Population Characteristics, Nebraska, 1990CP-1-29. Washington, DC: Government Printing Office, 1992.

Vehik, Susan C. Dhegiha Origins and Plains Archaeology. *Plains Anthropologist*. 38 (146): 231–252. 1993

Wishart, David J. *An Unspeakable Sadness: The Dispossession of the Nebraska Indians*. Lincoln: University of Nebraska Press, 1994.

Wissler, Clark, editor. *Societies of the Plains Indians*, Anthropological Papers of the American Museum of Natural History, Vol XI, New York: AMNH, 1916.

Contributors

Elmer Blackbird
Grace Blackbird
Minnie Davis Blackbird
William Canby
Alberta Grant Canby
Mary Hallowell Clay
Eddie Cline
Albert Dick
Louie Dick, Sr.
Margaret Wolfe Dick
Sarah Mitchell Dick
Jacob "Zac" Drum
Charles Edwards
Lavina Esau
Irene Harlan Gilpin
Joseph A. Gilpin
Kathryn Morris Gilpin
Lawrence Gilpin
Naomi Cline Gilpin
Florence White Grant
Ramona Turner Greany
Rose Wood Harlan
Ed Kemp
Susan Freemont
Richard Lovejoy
Morgan Lovejoy
Eva McCauley Mackey
John Michael Mangan
Jerry Maryott
Arthur T. May
George Mitchell
Bryan Morris

Elsie Gilpin Morris
Nellie Canby Morris
Donna Rae Morris Parker
Gertrude "Emily" Parker
Raymond Phillips, Sr.
Nora Pratt
Emmaline Walker Sanchez
Vera Grant Sheridan
Lizzie Lieb Springer
Charles Stabler, Jr.
Coolidge Stabler
Elizabeth Saunsoci Stabler
Gertrude "Tiny" Robinson Stabler
Hollis D. Stabler, Jr.
Hollis D. Stabler, Sr.
Lorenzo Stabler
Lucille Thomas
Pauline McCauley Tyndall
Wayne Tyndall
Enos Walker
Thomas Carson Walker
Betsy Hastings White
Bertha McCauley Wolfe
Clifford Wolfe, Sr.
Lillian Dixon Wolfe

Index

Lightning Source UK Ltd.
Milton Keynes UK
UKOW02f0303181014

240248UK00012B/234/P

9 780803 217577